Creating
and Sharing
Online Library
Instruction

Creating and Sharing Online Library Instruction

A How-To-Do-It Manual for Librarians®

Joelle Pitts

Sara K. Kearns

Heather Collins

Neal-Schuman

An imprint of the American Library Association

Chicago   2017

Extensive effort has gone into ensuring the reliability of the information in this book; however, the publisher makes no warranty, express or implied, with respect to the material contained herein.

ISBN: 978-0-8389-1562-2 (paper)

Library of Congress Cataloging-in-Publication Data

Names: Pitts, Joelle, author. | Kearns, Sara K., author. | Collins, Heather, 1977– author.
Title: Creating and sharing online library instruction : a how-to-do-it manual for librarians / Joelle Pitts, Sara K. Kearns, Heather Collins.
Description: Chicago : ALA Neal-Schuman, an imprint of the American Library Association, 2017. | Series: A how-to-do-it manual for librarians | Includes bibliographical references and index.
Identifiers: LCCN 2017005082 | ISBN 9780838915622 (pbk. : alk. paper)
Subjects: LCSH: Academic libraries—Relations with faculty and curriculum. | Web-based instruction—Design. | Web-based instruction—Evaluation. | Information literacy—Study and teaching (Higher) | Information literacy—Web-based instruction. | Academic librarians—Professional relationships. | Academic libraries—Relations with faculty and curriculum—United States—Case studies. | Library cooperation—United States—Case studies.
Classification: LCC Z675.U5 P525 2017 | DDC 025.5/677—dc23 LC record available at https://lccn.loc.gov/2017005082

Cover images © Adobe Stock. Composition by Dianne M. Rooney in the Minion Pro and Interstate typefaces.

♾ This paper meets the requirements of ANSI/NISO Z39.48–1992 (Permanence of Paper).

Printed in the United States of America

21 20 19 18 17   5 4 3 2 1

Contents

Contents

Figures

Figures

Preface

Teaching our students and communities to think critically about the information they consume and create has never been harder. The information landscape continually evolves. Billions of gigabytes of data are created daily, and the contexts in which information is encountered come and go with dizzying speed. New challenges arrive faster and faster in the form of policy and administration changes, technological advances and practices, cultural norms, and even in our standard practices within the library profession. Even our definition of literacy is changing as we seek to enable our patrons to contribute meaningfully to their communities of practice, wherever they may be. If we as librarians try to manage teaching in this context by ourselves, we are easily overwhelmed with the pressure of keeping current despite limited resources.

This book is not a library instruction panacea, but it does offer a sustainable pathway toward achieving greater information literacy within and across communities. Using the principles of backward design and the rapid prototyping development model, this manual offers a shared vocabulary for librarians, instructional designers, and others to reference when developing online library instruction. We present a model for collaboratively building asynchronous online information literacy instruction that can be reused, repurposed, and remixed across classes, departments, colleges, and even institutions.

We have devoted several years to working through the intricacies of building asynchronous learning objects that will work at multiple institutions in multiple contexts. The result is the award-winning New Literacies Alliance (NLA) project. When writing this manual, we drew upon our years of experience developing both the collaboration and learning objects. We also drew upon our expertise in instructional design, library administration, distance curriculum design and coordination, and knowledge of educational theory and literacies. We believe strongly in the value of online education in its own right and have decades of library and distance education experience among us to support the practices, tips, and suggestions you will find in these pages.

We organized this manual to guide you through the decision-making processes of a collaboration, starting in chapter 1 with a discussion about the value of collaboratively creating online learning. Chapters 2 through 8 then walk you through the steps in collaborative learning object design. We provide concrete guidance as much as possible but recognize that time, technology, and the unique composition and goal of every collaboration would render prescribed instructions ineffectual. To aid in your project planning and implementation, therefore, chapters 2 through 8 also each include checklists of steps and lists of critical questions to help you make informed decisions for your project. Additionally, the manual includes concrete examples of successes and failures based on five years of effort on the NLA project.

The chapters build on each other but can be used independently. References are cited throughout the text so you can read more about foundational theories and practices. Although written for groups or individuals who want to collaborate to build learning objects, this book can be useful to anyone with a desire to learn more about instructional design, project planning, and library instruction. We hope this manual for collaborative learning object design helps you and your institutions save time and money, but more so, we hope this content helps you achieve a sustainable instructional model aimed at developing your patrons into critical, thoughtful citizens with skills to last them a lifetime.

Acknowledgments

The New Literacies Alliance is made possible and has been positively influenced by an extraordinarily dedicated and thoughtful group of librarians, administrators, designers, teachers, and students. We would like to take a moment to acknowledge them and their contributions.

Thank you to our project administrators, Lori A. Goetsch, Karen Cole, Steffani Webb, and Jameson Watkins, for inspiring and challenging us to make this venture a success. To Kristin Whitehair and Anne Huffman, founding team members, thank you for your early contributions. To our instructional designers, Alice Anderson, Cristina Colquhoun, and Eric Kowalik, and our instructional design residents, Marc Nash and Holger Lenz, thank you for your deep commitment to quality and user experience: our foundation would not be as strong without your hours and thoughtful planning and creative design. Thank you to our faculty and staff collaborators, Lorraine Buchanan, Sharon Kumm, Cindy Logan, Jennifer MacFadyen, Morgan Rakestraw, and Karen Tarnow, who shared with us your expertise and let us experiment with literacy instruction in a new way in your classes. Thank you to Debra Gilchrist, who provided early pedagogical advice and whose work still grounds this project. Thank you to our graphic designers, Tara Mosier and Amy Ritterskamp, who created our beautiful color palette and logo. Thank you to our fabulous student employees, Ashley Flinn, Hongmin Li, and Jessica Reyes, who provided artwork, code, and creativity that have helped our project flourish. Thank you to Shannon Hennessy for her project management. We also thank Lisa Loberg and Sara Motsinger, who have helped us navigate large-group logistics.

Finally, to all of the talented librarians who have contributed untold hours to New Literacies Alliance content, assessment, planning, and structure over the years—Andrea Baer, Tara Baillargeon, Melia Fritch, Cynthia Garrety, Robyn Hartman, Heather Healy, Geoffrey Iverson, Holly Luetkenhaus, Christina Magnifico, Kate Otto, Sara Robertson, Ashley Stark, Matt Upson, Rachel Vukas, and Julie Hartwell—thank you.

We are so grateful for your ideas, contributions, and dedication to the project over the years. Thank you for making this work so truly enjoyable, rewarding, and valuable.

The Case for Sharing Instruction

1

TERMS

Asynchronous learning   Environments in which learners can access remote learning resources using relatively inexpensive equipment to learn at home, at the workplace, or at any place of their choosing, at any time of their choosing (modified from Mayadas 1997). Usually, the term is used to describe online lessons or activities that can be independently completed outside a scheduled class meeting time.

Instructional design   The systematic and reflective process of translating principles of learning and instruction into plans for instructional materials, activities, information resources, and evaluation (Smith and Ragan 2005).

Learning object   A collection of content items, practice items, and assessment items that are combined based on a single learning objective (modified from Hodgins 2000).

Alone we are smart but together we are brilliant. We can use the collective wisdom to do great things when we are connected.

—Steven W. Anderson (2013)

Librarianship is both a solitary and a cooperative profession, particularly for academic librarians who provide instruction. We create student learning activities to address the needs of "our" students in engineering or philosophy or marketing and yet recognize that the librarian in the next office or down the road is developing resources to teach many of the same concepts. We share best practices on e-mail lists and at conferences and even collaborate in the classroom.

Yet, some of us still wonder, *Why are we all creating the same content?* Would it be more efficient to share and reuse basic instructional resources so we can focus our time on developing content that is more discipline-specific or that challenges students to higher levels of critical thinking? We think it would be, and we have done it. This manual describes how librarians and instructional designers can collaborate to create learning objects that can be reused among librarians in one institution or across multiple institutions.

Learning Object Design in Libraries

Learning object design for library instruction can be traced back at least several decades to the development of library "pathfinders" in the early 1950s (Vileno 2007). Pathfinders, also known as subject guides, began as brief, annotated paper handouts guiding researchers to library materials on specific topics. The Internet led to electronic versions of pathfinders being posted on library websites and an increased emphasis on creating static online instructional content to teach patrons how to use the library (Vileno 2007). Instructional design in libraries built momentum in the early 2000s with the creation of the first Instructional Design Librarian positions at colleges and universities (Shank 2006) and the creation of the Blended Librarians Online Learning Community (http://blendedlibrarian.learning times.net) by Steven Bell and John Shank. The growing number of distance education students, nontraditional students, and changing technological preferences spurred this growing group of blended librarians to recognize and assert a need for more diverse instructional offerings for our patrons. Yet, library instructional design expertise is still a finite resource in most libraries, even in higher education.

Large academic libraries may employ one or two instructional design staff to create learning experiences and what we will refer to in this manual as *learning objects*. We use *learning object* throughout this manual because it is a useful umbrella term that encompasses lessons, tutorials, videos, guides, and a myriad of other reusable instruction projects. Library learning object examples include LibGuides, database videos, assignment calculators, video walkthroughs, and other asynchronous online learning content that library patrons can access and engage with on their own time using their own devices. Learning objects may be one discrete item or a package comprised of videos, assessment activities, and reflective questions. Effective library learning objects can be reused, repurposed, and shared among institutional colleagues and beyond. Feel free to mentally insert your own project type (tutorial, learning resource, knowledge object, lesson, etc.) in place of *learning object* throughout this manual.

Cooperative Library Instruction Projects

As early as 1969, an effort to create cooperative pathfinders, Massachusetts Institute of Technology's Library Pathfinder, attempted to address limited library resources and overlaps in research services (Stevens, Canfield, and Gardner 1973). The Library Pathfinder program featured a systematic approach to developing pathfinders at multiple institutions with the intent to meet a common standard of quality, keep the pathfinders updated, and distribute pathfinders to interested institutions. The project coordinators soon found that other librarians welcomed premade pathfinders but were more inclined to pay for them than to contribute their own.

Librarians continue to be, at their core, a sharing and collaborative bunch of people. Many share their instruction ideas through peer-reviewed or open-access sites, including these:

- Community of Online Research Assignments (CORA), www.projectcora.org
- PRIMO: Peer-Reviewed Instructional Materials Online Database, http://primodb.org

State and regional initiatives arose to create tutorials and, in some cases, make the tutorials available outside of the collaboration. The TRAILS (Tool for Real-time Assessment of Information Literacy Skills, www.trails-9.org), TILT (Texas Information Literacy Tutorial, library.uno.edu/helpfiles/TILT/ and library.cypresscollege.edu/tilt/tilt.html), and CLIP (Cooperative Library Instruction Project, www.clipinfolit.org) projects are three such examples (CLIP and TILT are no longer active). Many similar collaborative efforts grappled with technology changes, staff members moving to new institutions, and grants ending; effectively shuttering or leaving collaborative projects in limbo. Additionally, previous efforts to form interinstitutional collaborations around library instruction typically focused on stand-alone tutorials that could be embedded and used by anyone, but these lacked a means to systematically gather student learning assessment data at the project level (Atwater-Singer and Metcalf 2006).

The advent of the Association of College & Research Libraries' (ACRL 2016) *Framework for Information Literacy for Higher Education (Framework)* has also challenged the way librarians traditionally deliver library instruction. Truly addressing the scope of information literacy and critical thinking in context is difficult to accomplish in library one-shot sessions. The Framework encourages the library profession to seek more in-depth and reflective modalities to improve student learning. Although many projects are currently in the works, few collaborative efforts to build asynchronous learning objects based on the *Framework* are underway. The New Literacies Alliance (NLA) is a notable exception.

New Literacies Alliance

Kansas State University Libraries (K-State) and The University of Kansas Medical Center Dykes Library (KUMC) formed the NLA collaboration in 2012. We came together when our dean and director recognized that the development of online learning objects at our respective institutions would be more effective as a collaborative effort. Through our work in, variously, health sciences and instructional design and with first-year college students, we became aware that the evolution of online environments meant our students were constantly immersed in information, and as likely to be authors of information as they were consumers. We wanted to create information literacy learning objects that addressed the new literacies needed to navigate various online environments. While the developing theory of new literacies is explored in a variety of fields (Coiro et al. 2008; Gee 2007; Lankshear and Knobel 2007; Wilber 2008), Mackey and Jacobson's (2011) concept of metaliteracies allowed us to stay rooted in information literacy:

> Metaliteracy is an overarching, self-referential, and comprehensive framework that informs other literacy types. Information literacy is the metaliteracy for a digital age because it provides the higher order thinking required to engage with multiple document types through various media formats in collaborative environments. (70)

We anticipated that learning experiences underlined by metaliteracy would guide our students beyond the behavioral elements of learning (what we want students to be able to do after an instructional experience) to reach the affective, cognitive, and metacognitive elements of learning that are critical to long-term retention and transfer of concepts. The interweaving of information literacy, new literacies, and metaliteracies was so foundational to our project that we chose the name New Literacies Alliance to reflect the new literacies encompassed by metaliteracy.

NLA's early work focused on digital literacy content and shifted to building learning objects based on knowledge practices in the new *Framework* shortly after the official document was released. Because NLA already incorporated many of the foundational underpinnings of the *Framework* (metaliteracy, backward design, critical thinking, etc.), our efforts dovetailed almost perfectly with the *Framework*'s focus on new ways of teaching information literacy to college students.

NLA has since grown to include nine member libraries, and our lessons, which are available under a Creative Commons license, have been used at more than a dozen universities. NLA won the 2016 ACRL Instruction Section Innovation Award. We welcome new partners and users and hope to see many more collaborations develop.

Why Collaborate

The case for sharing library instruction can be made on several levels. The first level is the need to maximize our resources and time to create the most meaningful learning experiences we can. Why re-create the wheel at every college and university when a streamlined collaboration can accomplish more when partners bring unique talents, software, stakeholders, and ideas to the table? Second, collaborating helps us see the broader information

---

BROADER PICTURE OF METALITERACY INSTRUCTION

In the short term, metaliteracy instruction is a strategy to enhance overall academic success. Metaliteracy is "learning how to learn" (Mackey and Jacobson 2011), so it follows that students who are metaliterate will be more successful in their professional and personal lives. The broader goal of information literacy instruction is to empower all students with this ability. Many institutions are now weaving information literacy instruction into student success initiatives. The intent is that metaliteracy instruction, delivered more broadly online to as many students as possible, can act as a leveling platform for students facing socioeconomic, cultural, experiential, or academic disadvantages.

literacy landscape, to contextualize the needs of our students and communities. We should always strive to tailor our instruction, programming, and efforts to meet the needs of our own local stakeholders, but the reality is that our students are mobile and connected. Students work toward a degree by taking classes at multiple institutions and seeking out resources to help them learn content, no matter who created it. The last and perhaps most obvious reason to collaborate is the capacity and affinity for open information practices within the library profession. Like no other industry or community, librarians are uniquely wired to collaborate to help people learn about information.

The following chapters will use the NLA as a lens through which to showcase shareable learning design, and we hope that whether you are designing library instruction as a group of two or three at a small college or planning to create a large interinstitutional library instruction collaborative like the NLA, the chapters in this manual will help you get started.

CRITICAL QUESTIONS

1. Do you have the staffing, expertise, time, and other resources to create library instruction on your own?
2. Will it benefit your library/institution/patrons to collaborate on library instruction?
3. What are the barriers to collaboration that you foresee?

References

ACRL (Association of College & Research Libraries). 2016. *Framework for Information Literacy for Higher Education.* Chicago: American Library Association. www.ala.org/acrl/standards/ilframework.

Anderson, Steven W. 2013. Twitter post, September 17, 4:12 p.m. https://twitter.com/web20classroom.

Atwater-Singer, Meg, and Susan Metcalf. 2006. "The Begetting of Information Literacy Tutorials: Third-Wave Tutorials for the iPod Generation." In *Moving Targets: Understanding Our Changing Landscapes* (LOEX Conference Proceedings), edited by Theresa Valko and Brad Sietz, 59–62. Ypsilanti, MI: Eastern Michigan University. http://commons.emich.edu/loexconf2006.

Coiro, Julie, Michelle Knobel, Colin Lankshear, and Donald J. Leu. 2008. "Central Issues in New Literacies and New Literacies Research." In *Handbook of Research on New Literacies*, edited by Julie Coiro, Michelle Knobel, Colin Lankshear, and Donald J. Leu, 1–21. New York: Lawrence Erlbaum, Taylor & Francis.

Gee, James. 2007. *Good Video Games + Good Learning: Collected Essays on Video Games, Learning and Literacy.* New York: Peter Lang.

Hodgins, Wayne. 2000. "Into the Future: A Vision Paper." Paper prepared for the American Society for Training and Development and National Governors' Association, Commission on Technology and Adult Learning. http://citeseerx.ist.psu.edu/viewdoc/summary?doi=10.1.1.87.8864.

Lankshear, Colin, and Michelle Knobel. 2007. "Sampling 'The New' in New Literacies." In *New Literacies Sampler*, edited by Michelle Knobel and Colin Lankshear, 1–24. New York: Peter Lang.

Mackey, Thomas P., and Trudi E. Jacobsen. 2011. "Reframing Information Literacy as Metaliteracy." *College & Research Libraries* 72 (1): 62–78. http://dx.doi.org/10.5860/crl-76r1.

Mayadas, Frank. 1997. "Asynchronous Learning Networks: A Sloan Foundation Perspective." *Journal of Asynchronous Learning Networks* 1 (1): 1–16.

Shank, John D. 2006. "The Blended Librarian: A Job Announcement Analysis of the Newly Emerging Position of Instructional Design Librarian." *College & Research Libraries* 67 (6): 515–24. http://dx.doi.org/10.5860/crl.67.6.514.

Smith, P. L., and T. Ragan. 2005. *Instructional Design.* Hoboken, NJ: Wiley.

Stevens, Charles H., Marie P. Canfield, and Jeffrey J. Gardner. 1973. "Library Pathfinders: A New Possibility for Cooperative Reference Service." *College & Research Libraries* 34 (1): 40–46. crl.acrl.org/content/34/1/40.full.pdf. http://crl.acrl.org/index.php/crl/article/view/12490/13936.

Vileno, Luigina. 2007. "From Paper to Electronic, the Evolution of Pathfinders: A Review of the Literature." *Reference Services Review* 35 (3): 434–51.

Wilber, Dana J. 2008. "College Students and New Literacy Practices." In *Handbook of Research on New Literacies*, edited by Julie Coiro, Michelle Knobel, Colin Lankshear, and Donald J. Leu, 553–81. New York: Lawrence Erlbaum, Taylor & Francis.

Getting Started

Preparation, I have often said, is rightly two-thirds of any venture.

—Amelia Earhart (1937)

Beginning in this chapter and continuing through chapter 8, this manual outlines the logistics of planning for collaborations, creation of learning experiences, designing and marketing learning objects, implementing learning objects, technical parameters, assessment, and long-term planning. We created a master checklist of the steps and critical questions to consider at each phase in the process (see appendix I). You might find it helpful to remove that list from the end of the book and keep it nearby as you move through each chapter.

This chapter helps you first determine if you need to enter into a collaboration. If you decide to pursue a collaboration, or if your administration has already determined a collaboration is necessary, we offer a blueprint for establishing a collaboration.

In This Chapter

✓ Determining the Need for a Collaboration

✓ Establishing a Collaboration

✓ Getting Started in Practice

CHECKLIST

☐ Conduct a self-study.

☐ Research existing collaborations.

☐ Identify and contact potential collaborators.

☐ Establish project goals.

☐ Confirm collaborator expectations.

☐ Identify leaders.

Determining the Need for a Collaboration

Instruction collaborations are an attractive idea, especially to librarians who, as a profession, lean toward the sharing economy and often work with limited resources. When we identify a common goal, pooling our efforts can seem like the next logical step. Before starting a collaboration, though, take some time to weigh the practicalities of collaborating to create learning objects: conduct a self-study, consider the benefits and constraints of collaborating, research existing collaborations, and identify potential partners.

Conduct a Self-Study

A self-study allows you to examine your own program and resources. If you already have potential collaborators, ask each to answer the following questions:

> What are your instruction goals?
>
> What goals can you not meet on your own?
>
> How flexible are your goals?
>
> Is there enough leeway to accommodate the instruction needs of other institutions (e.g., student learning outcomes, timelines, information technology [IT], funding)?
>
> How would working with other institutions help you achieve your instruction goals?
>
> How could you contribute to a collaboration?
>
> Does your library and/or university administration support interinstitutional collaborations?
>
> Are there constraints at your institution (e.g., IT, fiscal, human resources) that limit your ability to collaborate?

Knowing what you can bring to a project facilitates conversations within your institution and with potential collaborators. Be clear on what gaps exist in your efforts or goals to create learning objects and why you cannot fill those gaps within your own organization. See appendix A for the NLA self-study form distributed to potential collaborators in 2012.

Consider the Benefits and Constraints of Collaborating

In light of your self-study, consider the following questions: What benefits are most relevant? What constraints make a collaboration prohibitive?

Benefits of Collaborations

- Minimal duplication of work
- Maximized access to unique or expensive resources
- Maximized access to expertise
- Maximized production of learning objects
- Sharing of costs
- Development of professional relationships

Constraints of Collaborations

- Equal or increased commitment of staff time
- Establishing accountability across institutions
- Complexities of interinstitutional goal setting
- Incompatible technology
- Logistics of sharing costs

Research Existing Collaborations

Before building a collaboration from scratch, learn if there is an existing instruction project that meets your needs. When examining an existing collaboration consider these questions:

- Does it meet your project goals?
- How would it impact your pedagogy?
- Is the technology compatible with your institution's?
- Is the collaboration accepting new members?
- What would you be expected to contribute?
- What could you contribute?
- How active and/or productive is the collaboration?

Beyond the standard Internet search and literature review, identify collaborations by exploring the following:

- PRIMO submissions (http://primodb.org)
- Conference presentations, including poster sessions
- National, regional, and discipline-specific library associations
- The ACRL *Framework for Information Literacy* Sandbox (http://sandbox.acrl.org)

Whether joining an existing project or forming your own collaboration, your administrators will want to know that you have done your due diligence before contributing resources to a project.

Identify Potential Collaborators

If you determine that a collaboration is right for your project and you do not already have collaborators in mind, use the project goals identified in the self-study as parameters to search for potential collaborators. Start with those whom you know through professional memberships, conferences, or prior collaborations. Ask colleagues at your library, particularly your dean or director, for recommendations. Additionally, your library may already be a member of an instruction consortium that can be leveraged. Other ways to locate potential partners include these approaches:

- Conduct a literature review
- Attend conferences

- Join professional associations
- Post feelers on electronic discussion lists or social media

Geography is diminishing as a barrier for collaborations. Advances in communication technology, collaboration software, and the shift to cloud computing mean that you rarely, if ever, need to meet in person. NLA's working group has members at almost ten institutions in eight states who regularly meet using videoconferencing software and collectively edit documents using Google Docs. Team members across the country virtually attend our day-long planning retreats and even participate in breakout sessions. Unless location is a key aspect of your project, be adventurous and seek collaborators far and wide.

Make the Decision

Now that you have conducted an analysis of the environment, review the data and ask these questions:

- Do we share goals with anyone else?
- Can we combine resources with anyone else in a meaningful way?
- Together, do we have the right skills and personnel to achieve our goals?

Establishing a Collaboration

Building a collaboration is an exercise in communication and project management. Have a clear idea about why you are bringing different institutions together, but also leave space for the project team to establish common goals. While establishing a collaboration does not have to happen in exactly this order, these steps do allow for a progression in decision making:

1. Invite collaborators.
2. Establish goals.
3. Identify roles to be filled.
4. Confirm collaborator expectations.

Invite Collaborators

When contacting potential partners, be prepared to communicate your goals, why you are seeking a collaboration, and, most importantly, why you are reaching out to that institution. There may be several levels in the communication process, starting at the librarian-to-librarian level and working up to library deans and directors. As brilliant as your project is, not every library contacted will be willing or able to join a collaboration. This is not necessarily a judgment on the quality of your project, but do listen for concerns, particularly if they are raised repeatedly. Unless there are specific reasons not to, invite more institutions than you actually think you will need to account for inevitable attrition.

Establish Goals

Whether interested institutions come together under a mandate or because they share interests, establish clear goals for the project. Assuming everyone is on the same page can cause confusion and working at cross-purposes in the long term.

Establishing goals can be time-intensive, but it is possible to accomplish this efficiently. Set aside *at least* a full day to facilitate the discussion in real time. Discussing goals via e-mail or in other asynchronous environments reduces the quality of the discussion. Ask participants to come prepared with answers to specific questions, such as those asked in the self-study. Whether an in-person meeting or a videoconference, ensure that all participants have the opportunity to present their answers and to ask questions of one another. Exercises like Liberating Structures' "1-2-4-All" or "Purpose-to-Practice" (www.liberatingstructures.com) focus the discussion, provide opportunities for all participants to share ideas, and promote efficiently reaching a consensus.

Establish the goals or parameters of your project to include the following:

- Audience
- Student learning outcomes
- Implementation model
- Project deliverables

Some of these parameters may seem obvious based on the institutions brought together, but discussing, agreeing upon, and recording these parameters will streamline future decision making.

Audience Who will learn from the learning objects? Are you focusing on students in a certain discipline, students at particular types of institutions, certain demographics of students? Even if your audience is broad (all students in higher education), discuss and record your decision.

Student learning outcomes What will students be able to accomplish when they finish your learning objects? You do not need to draft outcomes for all learning objects at this point, but you should be able to define the overarching student learning that should occur.

Implementation model How will the learning objects be integrated into student learning? Many possible models exist, including these:

À la carte   Learning objects are used as needed in courses, on course research guides, and as compilations of FAQs (frequently asked questions). Each learning object can stand alone or be packaged with others.

Programmatic   Learning objects are embedded into an existing curriculum as part of a degree requirement.

Institutional   Learning objects are an entrance, a graduation, or another requirement for all students at an institution.

Certificate   Students who successfully complete learning objects receive a record of certification that may or may not be required or recognized by an institution or professional body.

Consortial   Learning objects are required of all students represented by a consortium. This may work best when the collaboration is comprised of institutions within a particular university system or with a shared governing body.

It is possible within a collaboration to have any or all of these implementation levels occur. Whether this is feasible will depend on your other goals, planning, and technology decisions. The more buy-in or approval needed from people outside the project team to implement the learning objects, the more regulations and rules the project will need to adhere to. See chapter 5, "Implementation," for more information.

Project deliverables   What will the final product look like? Again, you do not need to have precise details, but consider how the learning objects will be packaged and delivered to the student. Establish deadlines so that participants understand how long they are committing resources to the project.

Identify Roles to Be Filled

Interinstitutional projects to develop online learning objects can be as small as one librarian each from two institutions working on a project or as large as dozens of librarians and professional staff from numerous institutions. No matter the size, certain types of work need to be done in order to accomplish a project. This section discusses some of the most important roles to be filled. A project may assign separate individuals to each role, but it is also very common to have members of a project filling multiple roles. When planning, outline the roles that are necessary and have institutions identify which ones they can fill.

Steering Committee

The steering committee ultimately keeps the project moving forward. The committee works with a deans and/or directors sponsors group, planning the growth and sustainability of the project up to five years in advance. Members may have the ability to encumber resources, such as staff time or technology, from their institutions. The steering committee can include a representative of each institution involved in the project or a smaller cohort representing highly invested partners. See appendix B for more details on steering committee responsibilities.

Project Manager

A project manager leads the project from inception to completion, keeping the team focused on goals and deadlines. The project manager should be a member of the steering committee to avoid confusion in leadership. Project management requires a significant time investment, so the position description for the person serving in this role should include this responsibility in order to encumber the person's time.

Deans and Directors Sponsors Group

Comprised of deans and/or directors from member institutions, this group provides leadership for the steering committee, advising on infrastructure, scope, and targeted user groups through regular meetings. Group members identify and encumber resources and communicate with fellow deans and directors. The deans and directors sponsors group may represent every institution or a select smaller group. The sponsors hold the project accountable to goals and deadlines.

Instructional Designer/
Instructional Design Librarian

Instructional designers or instructional design librarians have training and/or experience in designing learning objects in online environments. Their experience with online learning, design tools, writing for the Web, and accessibility ensure that the learning objects will be usable. The instructional designer transforms content developed by the content creators into online learning objects. Because online learning objects require so much technical and design knowledge, an instructional design librarian should be central to any interinstitutional online learning object collaboration.

The number of instructional designers and their workload capacity dictate how many learning objects can be created. Instructional designers can come from multiple institutions, and they must be able to access the lesson creation software.

Content Creators

Content creators may be librarians, teaching partners (instructors or faculty who teach courses that will use the learning objects), or other educators. Content creators provide discipline expertise, in this case with information literacy. Their contributions include the following:

- Knowledge of how information literacy and related concepts are currently taught

One of the most important aspects of project management is the need for a project sponsor. Many projects fail because of either the lack of a sponsor or a sponsor who is either inactive or uninvolved.

—Shannon Hennessy, Project Manager, KUMC (pers. comm.)

- Knowledge of gaps or needs in information literacy instruction
- Developing learning objects, particularly the student learning outcomes
- Collaborating with instructional designers and/or instructional design librarians to develop assessments and learning experiences
- Reviewing learning objects
- Implementing learning objects

Content creators can come from multiple universities, but they do not necessarily need to have access to the lesson creation software. Institutions without technology resources can still actively participate in collaborations by involving content creators.

Future Roles

As the project develops, other roles will arise to address particular needs, which may include these:

- Assessment
- Programming/systems administration/IT
- Technical writing/editing
- Graphic design
- Public relations (PR)/marketing
- Budgets/accounting

The NLA uses a working group and adjunct model (see figure 2.1). The deans and directors sponsors group oversees the project by providing a big-picture perspective and allocating resources as necessary. The working group, at the core of the project, includes those roles that are central to the project's development; people in these roles participate in monthly meetings, serve on teams, and contribute to decisions about the project's development. We turn to adjunct partners, such as programmers and graphic designers, for specific expertise; they contribute their expertise as needed but do not assist with the ongoing development and planning. Finally, we turn to professionals like grant writers for external expertise. Because they are not involved in the design and implementation of the lessons, but aid us in endeavors to advance the project, they are situated outside the working group like satellites. As the project develops, we may add additional roles to the working group. For instance, once we had lessons in active use, we added an assessment role to the working group. As more people join our collaboration and fill various roles, members of our steering committee, who once filled every role, can now focus their efforts in a couple of areas.

When a collaboration is small, individuals assume multiple roles or you can "borrow" colleagues from within your institution for discrete aspects of the project. NLA collaborated with K-State's graphic designer to create our style guide but does not have a graphic designer permanently on the team. Larger collaborations mean participants can focus on fewer roles. You can

FIGURE 2.1

Working Group and Adjunct Model

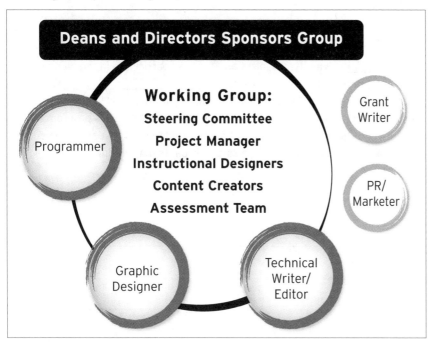

also grow a collaboration by welcoming an institution who can contribute the time of, say, a technical writer to review lessons for online readability but otherwise does not have the human resources to commit to the project. NLA keeps an updated list of project needs so that when we are contacted, we can easily work with potential collaborators to identify ways they can contribute.

Confirm Collaborator Expectations

Unless the participants in the discussion have the authority to make decisions about encumbering resources and joining the project, they probably need approval from their institutions. Institutions can respond to the proposed project in a variety of ways:

- Agreeing to the project goals and commit resources
- Asking that the goals be modified before committing resources
- Deciding that they cannot commit to the project due to lack of interest or resources

When institutions agree to the goals and to join the project, this is best laid out formally. Some projects use documents like an Intent to Plan or a Memorandum of Agreement to record the project goals and responsibilities of members and to ask institutions to detail the resources they can commit. This documentation provides clarity for future decisions and an understanding about what resources have been encumbered. Some institutions who

FIGURE 2.2

Intent to Plan Excerpt

It is understood that additional parties may be invited to join this cooperative effort.

_____University/organization agrees to participate in the planning process. By affixing the appropriate signatures to this document,_____ Library/organization agrees to support faculty participating in the planning of the digital instruction program. A Memorandum of Agreement pertaining to the delivery and maintenance of this program will be created between the Consortium and the University/organization. It is understood that at any time in the planning process or at the conclusion of the planning process, participants may withdraw from the program initiative.

Signatures   **Date**

Program Faculty _____

Program Department Head _____

Library/Organization Administrator _____

---

want to join the collaboration are unwilling or unable to sign a document that is legally binding. Work with the project sponsors to determine how binding the agreement to collaborate needs to be.

When NLA formed under the auspices of the Kansas Council of Deans and Directors of Libraries, our first objective was to explore the possibility of creating a statewide digital instruction program. Interested institutions signed an Intent to Plan document (see appendix C), an excerpt of which appears in figure 2.2. This primarily allowed the deans and directors to hold one another's institutions accountable to the project. Now when a librarian from a new institution joins NLA, one or more of our sponsors reach out to the librarian's dean or director to elaborate on the project, confirm expectations, and clarify commitments.

Getting Started in Practice

The NLA collaboration began when librarians at KUMC and K-State recognized a common objective. Both institutions needed to expand in-person and online instruction in order to reach more students. Additionally, most learning resources concentrated on basic information literacy skills and did not allow librarians to engage with students on higher-level or discipline-specific literacies. The KUMC team recognized the need for engaging, interactive, and scored tutorials; however, they struggled to evolve the learning objects beyond narrated PowerPoint presentations, live Adobe

Connect work sessions, and hyperlinked resources. Meanwhile, an interdepartmental team at K-State created online learning objects that could be reused in multiple courses and contexts. K-State had the staff to maintain existing in-person instruction and basic learning objects but not to develop higher-level learning objects.

The dean and director of the two libraries recognized that the work would be more effective as a cooperative effort and sought to establish a statewide collaboration. Other institutions were interested but asked KUMC and K-State to create a proof of concept (POC). A four-person team comprised of two librarians each from K-State and KUMC identified two outcomes necessary for a successful POC: collaboratively created learning objects and the foundations for a collaborative project.

The team spent the next eighteen months creating POC learning objects. Without an existing framework for our collaboration, much of the work involved learning how to work with one another to design learning objects. The three of us who were not instructional designers found ourselves on a steep learning curve to create online learning objects, so we developed extensive documentation to guide ourselves and future partners through the design process. We established pedagogical goals, project parameters, a technology platform, and design principles so that the lessons could be reused across institutions. We determined that the project needed to do the following:

- Focus on metaliteracies in addition to the traditional information literacy standards.
- Assess student learning.
- Be technology-, vendor-, and institution-agnostic.
- Offer engaging content with interactive elements in a mobile-friendly environment.
- Remove or reduce the need to re-create the wheel at every institution.
- Produce Creative Commons–licensed content.

However, eighteen months was too long to create a POC. What our colleagues across the state wanted was a demonstration that librarians could collaboratively create a collection of learning objects more effectively than could individual institutions. Unfortunately, when reaching out to potential partners, we overwhelmed them with documentation and principles related to the collaboration, obscuring the value of the lessons. Possible partners were turned off by the seeming enormity of the collaboration.

The project team and our dean and director at KUMC and K-State Libraries engaged in a series of conversations to confirm our commitment, assess the program, and determine how to proceed. We recognized that we had "planned big" rather than nimbly. The breakthrough moment came with a question from project sponsor Jameson Watkins to the project team: What could we produce in six months that would be a minimum viable product, one that was beyond a proof of concept but that demonstrated a more streamlined approach with a rolling development schedule of smaller, more achievable releases?

When we shifted our focus to the learning objects, rather than the collaboration, more partners were willing to join us. While our consortial materials still inform NLA's long-term planning, having some flexibility in our collaborative structure has been best for the long term, particularly as we are not a prescribed consortium but continually welcome partners. A key takeaway from our experience is to concentrate on the outcome rather than the means. While setting the foundation was important, the POC team attempted to resolve any issue that might arise in the future with rules and made the error of assuming that the difficulties the team encountered predicted all future difficulties. This meant that we had learning object design guidelines and a consortial structure that answered the needs of two institutions, instead of welcoming all partners. A more reasonable process would have been to focus on creating the POC lessons, documenting potential design and collaboration issues, and taking both to our state partners to inform the creation of a collaboration.

CRITICAL QUESTIONS

1. What are your goals?
2. Are your goals flexible enough to accommodate the needs of other institutions?
3. How would working with other institutions help you achieve your goals?
4. How could you contribute to a collaboration?
5. Does your library and/or university administration support interinstitutional collaborations?
6. Can you share resources across institutions?
7. Is there an existing project that meets your needs that you can join?
8. Can you combine resources with anyone else in a meaningful way?
9. Who is the audience for the learning objects?
10. What will students be able to accomplish when they finish your learning objects?
11. How will the learning objects be integrated into student learning?
12. What will the final product look like?
13. What roles do you need to fill on your project?
14. Who will lead your project?

Reference

Earhart, Amelia. 1937. *Last Flight*. New York: Harcourt Brace.

Creating the Learning Experience

3

In This Chapter

✓ Teamwork
✓ Backward Design
✓ Online Lesson Planning in Practice

CHECKLIST

☐ Identify content creators.
☐ Organize teams.
☐ Select guiding activities for teams.
☐ Choose a pedagogical approach.
☐ Select an outcomes formula.
☐ Identify competencies.
☐ Set the structure of learning objects (templates).
☐ Customize an evaluation rubric.
☐ List creatable learning activities.

The art of being taught is the art of discovery, as the art of teaching is the art of assisting discovery to take place.
—Mark Van Doren (1943)

This chapter describes how librarians and instructional designers create effective learning objects using the *Framework for Information Literacy for Higher Education* (ACRL 2016). Chapter 4, "The Design Process," focuses on the instructional design methods used to build the actual learning objects with which students will engage. Creating the learning experience is the heart of your collaboration. It is also an iterative process, so do not be dismayed if you revisit stages multiple times.

Before planning a specific learning object, members of the collaboration will need to chart a path and put in place parameters to facilitate teamwork. Once that work is done, content creation teams can focus on developing specific learning objects using McTighe and Wiggins's (2012) "backward design" curriculum planning model.

Teamwork

Leadership is responsible for creating an environment where expertise and enthusiasm thrive, while at the same time avoiding the trappings of committee compromise, mediocrity, and divergent directions.

Shared Vision

Online lesson planning requires the team to focus on a shared vision from the beginning. This vision should guide all decisions from every team member. Unlike traditional instruction that can be fairly easily edited without causing much inconvenience or expense for others, editing online lesson plans can undo the work of many. These teams are where a lot of your project's work actually happens, so you will want to ensure that they can function productively. Members of the team should be aware of deadlines, expectations, and the process that will be followed.

Typically, teams are comprised of at least a content creator and an instructional designer, but optimally, they also include other content creators, faculty, a graphic designer, and an editor or a reviewer. Instructional designers depend upon content creators' knowledge of *what* students need to learn; content creators depend upon instructional designers' knowledge of *how* learning occurs online.

Provide teams with models to follow, like sample learning objects and templates, and general directions for navigating exceptional circumstances. A team should focus on one learning outcome at a time to avoid scope creep and general confusion. Your directions should balance the need for structure with flexibility to enable creativity and originality.

Activities to Focus Teams

Your team will be more effective if you provide guided activities to foster communication and the creation process.

Liberating Structures (www.liberatingstructures.com) is a set of simple activities and rules that guide cooperation and bring out each team member's unique contributions. The website provides approximately thirty-three activities that can be chosen quickly and applied to the team's task at hand, either in person or virtually. Individuals facilitate activities; they do not "lead" them. These tools spur creativity and engage members while also providing the basic structure that enables the team to interact and come to consensus about vision, obstacles, or content creation (Lipmanowicz and McCandless 2017a). Without this structure, teams often flounder at key transition points, such as the brainstorm-to-execution phase or when two proposals seem equally good. Without structure, teams also struggle to bring forward quieter voices and to balance more vocal members' input.

Librarians have different ideas about which areas of the *Framework* should be developed, so the Liberating Structures activity "1-2-4-All" serves as a team consensus-building tool (Lipmanowicz and McCandless 2017b). The activity uses timed cycles for individuals, pairs, and small groups to complete collaboration tasks. By the end of the exercise, each team member has spoken multiple times, listened to colleagues, and agreed on a decision.

Backward Design

The key to creating learning objects that will be used and valued is connecting them to the competencies students need to meet. The *Framework* was strategically designed to dovetail with general higher education competencies (ACRL 2016). Creating a curriculum map of the various competencies and linking them to the *Framework* allows you to identify which areas of the *Framework* are most needed and should be prioritized. A curriculum map reinforces the fact that you are working in tandem with faculty on a clearly articulated and unified purpose. While the map is a useful communication and advocacy tool, with or without it, it is essential that you work closely with faculty to strategically identify areas of the curriculum where content will enhance or fill gaps. You will use this map (or your knowledge of curriculum needs) in the process of backward design (described in this section). Figure 3.1 shows an excerpt of a map linking the various competencies in medical education.

Backward design is a curriculum planning model that focuses on outcomes and how students demonstrate competency. Designed by McTighe and Wiggins (2012), backward design has three interrelated stages:

Stage 1—Identify desired results.

Stage 2—Determine assessment evidence.

Stage 3—Plan learning experiences and instruction.

FIGURE 3.1

Sample Curriculum Map Excerpt

Health Information Literacy Competencies				
Information Literacy (ACRL)	SoM	SoM Graduation Competencies	ACGME	ACGME Common Requirements
Knowledge Management				
Information Creation as Process				
KM-C1 Articulate the capabilities and constraints of various research and information creation processes as they relate to medical practice.	MK2	Provide evidence for their diagnostic and management decisions based on application of medical knowledge and clinical reasoning.	MK IV.A.5.b	Residents must demonstrate knowledge of established and evolving biomedical, clinical, epidemiological, and social-behavioral sciences, as well as the application of this knowledge to patient care.
	MK3	Scientifically appraise innovative concepts and practices for potential value in patient care.		

SOURCE: Vukas and Collins 2016.

FIGURE 3.2

Steps to Backward Design

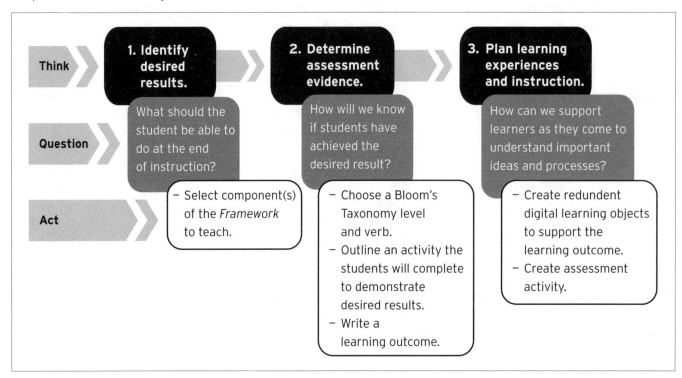

While McTighe and Wiggins apply their stages to a curriculum, we have found that the same stages (adapted slightly) work in designing learning objects (see figure 3.2).

Backward Design Stage 1: Identify Desired Results

> What should the student be able to do at the end of instruction?
> (McTighe and Wiggins 2012)

This is the most crucial and most difficult stage. You are establishing both the outcome and the scope of the learning object. The key to this stage is to identify what a student should be able to do, not what you will teach. Education and marketing researchers recommend retaining maximum engagement by keeping learning objects between eight and fifteen minutes long (Izenberg 2015).

Pull out your curriculum map, or at least the *Framework,* and begin selecting components to teach. As you do, note that some knowledge practices and dispositions from the *Framework* can be used as is, but they often require some customization. Here are some of the ways in which the NLA modified the *Framework* as we began using it as the basis of backward design.

FIGURE 3.3

Unpacking the *Framework*

Approach the Framework

The following knowledge practice covers a great deal of content: "Articulate the purpose and distinguishing characteristics of *copyright, fair use, open access,* and *the public domain*" (ACRL 2016; emphasis added). A more manageable outcome might simply be this: "Articulate the purpose and distinguish the characteristics of *copyright.*" Other modules focusing on fair use or open access or public domain could be created separately. Without being overly summative, it would be difficult in eight to fifteen minutes to meaningfully explore copyright, fair use, open access, *and* public domain.

Figure 3.3 illustrates highlighting a portion of the Framework—a knowledge practice or a disposition that is too big to cover in eight to fifteen minutes.

Highlight One Primary Frame

The *Framework* contains interrelated and overlapping content. Many concepts can be viewed through different "frames" (see figure 3.4). Sometimes you will want to teach a concept in the center of multiple overlapping areas. However, a learning object must focus on one outcome and be capable of being assessed and taught online. Exploring content through different frames is an excellent way to expand critical thinking as well as comprehension. You may choose to present the same content through different frames in subsequent learning objects or in-person instruction. Multiple frames may be cited as foundations for a particular learning object. However, when you write a learning outcome and design a learning object that can be taught and assessed in approximately eight to fifteen minutes, we advise sticking with one frame. By focusing on one frame, you can structure content clearly and concisely, providing a more direct path to comprehension.

As the NLA began working on a learning object focused on the "Scholarship as Conversation" frame, we found that the following knowledge practices (modified from the Framework) overlapped and could not be easily separated:

FIGURE 3.4

Overlapping Areas of the *Framework*

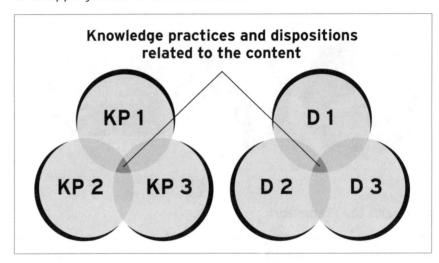

Conversation changes over time ("recognize they are often entering into an ongoing scholarly conversation and not a finished conversation")

Authority/who gets listened to ("recognize that systems privilege authorities[, which] disempowers [others'] ability to participate and engage")

You can join the conversation ("see themselves as contributors to scholarship rather than only consumers of it") (ACRL 2016)

We recognized that the learning object could touch on several knowledge practices and/or dispositions simultaneously. While we as the educators were aware that the learning object lay between three knowledge practices, for clarity, we gave our students only *one focused outcome*. The entire learning object was written around "Conversation changes over time" and referenced the other two knowledge practices only in the notes section (see figure 3.5).

Choose a Level

You can also customize a knowledge practice or disposition to various levels of expertise, creating lessons addressing the novice through to the expert, as shown in figure 3.6 (Dreyfus and Dreyfus 1980).

For example, in the frame "Searching as Strategic Exploration," knowledge practice five reads "design and refine needs and search strategies as necessary, based on search results" (ACRL 2016). You can target lower-level undergraduate students being exposed to the concept for the first time by introducing limits, controlled vocabulary, or the process of revising a basic search strategy. Alternatively, the concept can be expanded and taught at a much higher level, exploring discipline-specific strategies and/or advanced evidence-based practice research strategies.

TIP As you consider what students should be able to do, remember that the *Framework* expanded what is expected of students. They are required to be both consumers and creators of information within digital environments (ACRL 2016). Learning objects are far better environments than face-to-face instruction for students to learn and demonstrate this principle. By placing this content in learning objects, students are learning and demonstrating to you these abilities in the "natural environment."

FIGURE 3.5

Overlap versus User View

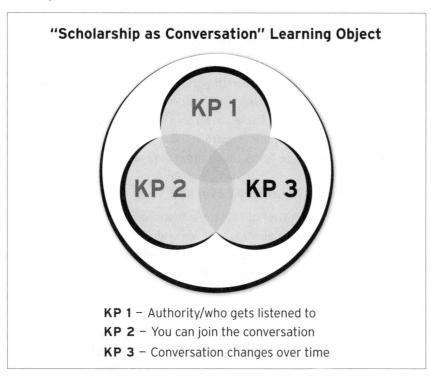

"Scholarship as Conversation" Learning Object

KP 1

KP 2   KP 3

KP 1 – Authority/who gets listened to
KP 2 – You can join the conversation
KP 3 – Conversation changes over time

FIGURE 3.6

Novice-to-Expert Steps

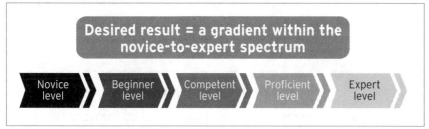

Desired result = a gradient within the novice-to-expert spectrum

Novice level → Beginner level → Competent level → Proficient level → Expert level

SOURCE: Dreyfus and Dreyfus 1980.

Backward Design Stage 2: Determine Assessment Evidence

> How will we know if students have achieved the desired results?
> (McTighe and Wiggins 2012)

In this stage, you must articulate what the students will do in order to demonstrate that they understand the content. Here it helps to envision what someone who understands the topic can do that others cannot. You will want students to show you that skill or behavior. Simply put, if you want to teach a student to ride a bike, you will know that the student has achieved the desired result when you see the student ride from point A to point B. The student's ride is the evidence.

TIP Those new to creating learning objects often gravitate to the lowest level of Bloom's Taxonomy, the "knowledge" level, when creating the foundational learning outcomes. Many people are used to learning object creation software being used to create matching, listing, definition, and labeling activities. The higher the Bloom's Taxonomy level, the more difficult it is to design online learning objects and activities, especially if automated grading is desired. Challenge yourself and your instructional designers! With creativity, even the simplest software activities can be adapted to address higher Bloom's Taxonomy levels. We promise it can be done!

TIP **What is the difference between an outcome and an objective?** The words **outcome** and **objective** are used in similar and sometimes interchangeable ways in educational parlance. However, "outcomes" describe what the student will be able to do after instruction and "objectives" refer to the actions and goals taken along the way. Learning outcomes often contain several objectives (Harden 2002).

In information literacy instruction, this stage requires librarians to create new knowledge by envisioning what the knowledge practices and dispositions of the *Framework* look like within various disciplines. Librarians are being called upon to articulate how a student has embraced threshold concepts or "portals to enlarged understanding or ways of thinking and practicing" (ACRL 2016). The *Framework* does not specifically tell you what evidence you should expect to see in performing arts students or biology students who have embraced the threshold concept and applied it to their subject area. Defining what these observable information practices are as they relate to specific disciplines is part of the cognitive work that information literacy librarians are being called upon to provide.

Choose a Bloom's Taxonomy Level and Verb

To begin, select the appropriate Bloom's Taxonomy level (see figure 3.7) and verb to describe how you anticipate observing proficiency (Bloom and Krathwohl 1956). Will the student simply label something (knowledge level) or will the student solve a problem (application level)?

Write a Learning Outcome

Remember that only one learning outcome should be used with an eight-to-fifteen-minute learning object (Izenberg 2015). There are many formulas and systems for writing outcome statements, but the Stiehl and Lewchuk (2008) model that is also used by Debra Gilchrist (2010) serves online learning object design especially well by forcing writers to articulate necessary components of the lesson plan early in the process. It also requires you to clearly state the assessment goal, which is important to backward design, as in the figure 3.8 example.

OUTCOME FORMULA

1. Begin with the phrase "The student will . . . ," which implies "by the end of the lesson." (Sometimes this is implied, but not written down.)
2. Add your selected Bloom's Taxonomy verb.
3. Add a short phrase describing the assessment evidence identified in stage 2 of backward design. (This is a short description of how you will observe the student demonstrating that he or she knows and can act on the information being taught.)
4. Add the phrase "in order to."
5. End with the desired results identified in stage 1 of backward design. This is the area of the *Framework* selected and the task that you want students to be able to do after completing the module.

Use the Outcomes Checklist on page 28 to review your completed outcome statement.

FIGURE 3.7

Bloom's Taxonomy

Level	Verbs	NLA Examples
1. **Knowledge** (Recall information.)	Define List Recognize Match Label Name Identify	Identify the characteristics of information in order to measure the value of information. Identify research strategies in order to discover more recent, contemporary contributions to a scholarly conversation.
2. **Application** (Apply knowledge or generalize to new situation.)	Apply Interpret Use Demonstrate Stretch Dramatize Illustrate Solve Prepare	Use the appropriate type of evidence (research studies) in order to address different types of clinical questions.
3. **Synthesis** (Bring together parts of knowledge to form a whole and build relationships for new situations.)	Arrange Create Prepare Compare Design Propose Conduct Organize Write	Construct a search strategy in order to use search tools more efficiently.
4. **Comprehension** (Interpret information in your own words.)	Classify Report Describe Select Discuss Translate	Make (select) informed decisions in order to anticipate the effects of access in your life and in the community.
5. **Analysis** (Break down knowledge into parts and show relationship among parts.)	Categorize Criticize Examine Compare Differentiate Question Contrast Discriminate Test	Compare two search outcomes in order to construct a search strategy. Differentiate between different digital formats in order to resolve your information need.

SOURCE: Modified from United States Geological Survey 1998.

FIGURE 3.8

Learning Outcome Formula

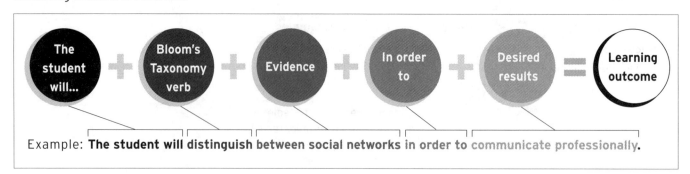

The student will... + Bloom's Taxonomy verb + Evidence + In order to + Desired results = Learning outcome

Example: **The student will distinguish** between social networks **in order to** communicate professionally.

OUTCOMES CHECKLIST

☐ *There is only one outcome per learning object.*

☐ *Outcome does not include multiple commas.* Multiple commas indicate an outcome that is too large. Lists are condensed into descriptive phrases.

☐ *Outcome follows the formula.* Outcomes should follow the sentence structure outlined in the Outcome Formula, including an appropriate Bloom's Taxonomy verb, evidence, "in order to" phrase, and desired results.

☐ *Bloom's Taxonomy verb is appropriate for the task.* The highest possible level of Bloom's Taxonomy is used.

☐ *Language is clear.* Outcomes should be understandable to all stake-holders in higher education, not just instructional librarians. Language should be simple and concise.

☐ *Outcome is realistic.* The scope of the content is appropriate for the time frame and audience.

☐ *The evidence and desired results are balanced.* The evidence that will be observed is appropriate considering the desired outcome. The evidence does not demand more than is necessary of the student, nor does it demand too little.

☐ *Outcome is measurable and assessable.* The outcome can be observed and measured. For example, if the student is supposed to "*match* A to B," that task can easily be both observed and graded. However, anticipating that the student "*understands* A and B" is not measurable or as-sessable. Most concretized outcomes can be graded through software.

NLA EXAMPLE

The student will be able to identify steps necessary in order to discover more recent contributions to the scholarly conversation about a topic.

Backward Design Stage 3:
Plan Learning Experiences

> How will we support learners as they come to understand important ideas and processes? (McTighe and Wiggins 2012)

Finally, after the outcome and assessment are written, it is time to create the learning object with its multiple activities. This is the time to unleash the creativity of the instructional designers and content writers. Using backward design (McTighe and Wiggins 2012) keeps the content focused on the outcome and ensures that the activities do not devolve into tangents. Avoid the temptation to incorporate a shiny new widget or a popular activity and then attempt to justify it by altering the outcome or assessment. Not only does this diverge from backward design; it also creates gaps in the lesson that frustrate the learning process.

Most instructional design software programs offer writers a common set of possible activities. However, activities vary from program to program and the skill of an instructional designer can greatly expand the types of activities that can be successfully deployed.

Common Instructional Design Program Activities

Drag and drop	Timeline or sequence	Photo album activity
Flashcards	Labeling	Quiz group
Matching	Sorting	Align activity
Multiple choice	Jigsaw puzzle	Identify activity
Fill in the blank	Ordering items	Selection activity
Match pairs	Slideshow	Charts activity
Crossword	Seek a word	

Learning Object Structure

NLA instructional designers developed a storyboard template to translate general lesson content into digital learning objects (Pitts, Lenz, and Nash 2013). Unlike in-person lectures or even online coursework, the writing for learning objects needs to be succinct and graphical, appropriate for screen reading. This storyboard template is meant to help you think through a learning object as it will appear online, and as the students will interact with it. It is meant to be a guide rather than a rule. If creating multiple learning objects, a template such as this provides uniformity that will aid students in navigation.

The storyboard template uses the formula for storytelling to deliver learning content (see figure 3.9). Both begin with an introduction that lays out the context. In literature, character development is established, and in the online lesson storyboard, definitions are provided and the concept is introduced. Then, the story rises and an activity, such as a reflective poll or

FIGURE 3.9

Instructional Design Story Arc

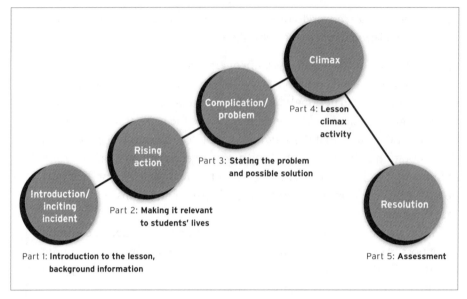

hypothetical situation, is introduced to make the content more relevant to the learner. In the introduction section, the problem is stated and instruction is given regarding the problem. The complication/problem section is where options are demonstrated for resolving the problem. Then, in the climax, the student is given the opportunity to practice solving the problem through an activity. Finally, in the resolution of the story, the main character (the learner) spends time reflecting on the journey or the content. This debriefing summarizes the content covered and is followed by some form of formative assessment (quiz questions, etc.).

The entire storyboard template appears as appendix D in this book.

Customization and Rearrangement

Technology allows for nuances in learning customization not possible in traditional face-to-face instruction. Students can self-select modules or pass through gated assessments that differentiate learners into an appropriate content level. Technology can also allow for students to "quiz out" of content and move on to other areas. Instructors are able to take apart online lessons and deliver components, such as a single quiz, a video, an activity, a reflection poll, and so on, independently or in different combinations. The possibilities for reusing content à la carte are endless.

Final Learning Object Rubric

When you finish the plans for your learning object, ask a peer to review it using the rubric provided in appendix E. Work with instructional designers and fellow content creators to move through the iterative creation process.

Online Lesson Planning in Practice

The NLA was among the first to write asynchronous online lessons based on the *Framework,* having focused first on metaliteracy instruction for nearly five years before the *Framework* was introduced. We found early work in this area to be challenging and rewarding. To create *Framework*-based learning objects, NLA members established a process. Two times a year, the entire group meets (at the beginning of each semester) to set goals for the upcoming semester and lay the groundwork for stage 1 of backward design by identifying competencies that will be used. The team also reflects on current and past work. During these meetings, smaller teams are formed to meet weekly throughout the semester to create the learning objects. Liberating Structures (www .liberatingstructures.com) are used to guide the meetings and team tasks.

Later, individuals volunteer to serve in small groups consisting of several content writers, at least one instructional designer, and a graphic artist. These small groups meet regularly to develop a learning outcome, sketch out a storyboard, and create the learning object. Teams meet weekly for approximately an hour throughout a semester to create a learning object. Near the end of the semester, lessons go through the rapid prototyping process (described in chapter 4) and proof editing prior to being published.

FINISHED NLA LESSONS

NLA learning objects are freely available for reuse under a Creative Commons Attribution-NonCommercial License. View, download, or obtain the code to embed the learning objects in a course management system from http://newliteraciesalliance.org.

CRITICAL QUESTIONS

1. Are team members clear about the central purpose and vision for the work?
2. Are teams facilitated with teamwork activities (Liberating Structures) to complete the work?
3. What is the student going to learn?
4. Why is this content important to the learners?
5. Will the content be covered broadly or in depth?
6. What audience level is targeted?
7. What specifically do you want students to be able to do *after* completing the learning object?
8. What skills or knowledge is necessary for the student to be a competent practitioner?
9. What level of mastery on the novice-to-expert scale (Dreyfus and Dreyfus 1980) is practically needed for this particular outcome and at this time?
10. How will you observe students demonstrating knowledge or understanding of this content? What evidence will best show you that they "got it"?
11. What online activities will you provide in the learning object to teach the content and prepare the student for the assessment?
12. What are the criteria for mastery? How will you know that the student has done this well or reached a level of proficiency?
13. Are the instructional librarians familiar with learning object writing styles and templates?

References

ACRL (Association of College & Research Libraries). 2016. *Framework for Information Literacy for Higher Education.* Chicago: American Library Association. www.ala.org/acrl/standards/ilframework.

Bloom, Benjamin Samuel, and David R. Krathwohl. 1956. *Taxonomy of Educational Objectives: The Classification of Educational Goals; Handbook 1.* New York: D. McKay.

Dreyfus, Stuart E., and Hubert L. Dreyfus. 1980. "A Five-Stage Model of the Mental Activities Involved in Directed Skill Acquisition." Operations Research Center Report. Berkeley: University of California. www.dtic.mil/docs/citations/ADA084551.

Gilchrist, Debra. 2010. "Assessment as Learning." Presentation at the University of Kansas Libraries Instruction Workshop, Lawrence, Kansas.

Harden, Ronald M. 2002. "Learning Outcomes and Instructional Objectives: Is There a Difference?" *Medical Teacher* 24 (2): 151–5.

Hodgins, Wayne. 2000. "Into the Future: A Vision Paper." Paper prepared for the American Society for Training and Development and National Governors' Association, Commission on Technology and Adult Learning. http://citeseerx.ist.psu.edu/viewdoc/summary?doi=10.1.1.87.8864.

Izenberg, Illysa. 2015. "The Eight-Minute Lecture Keeps Students Engaged." *Faculty Focus,* August 31. www.facultyfocus.com/articles/instructional-design/the-eight-minute-lecture-keeps-students-engaged.

Lipmanowicz, Henri, and Keith McCandless. 2017a. "Introduction." Liberating Structures. Accessed March 9. www.liberatingstructures.com.

———. 2017b. "1-2-4-All." Liberating Structures. Accessed March 6. www.liberatingstructures.com/1-1-2-4-all.

McTighe, Jay, and Grant Wiggins. 2012. "Understanding by Design® Framework." Overview report. Alexandria, VA: Association for Supervision and Curriculum Development. www.uab.edu/elearning/images/facultytoolkit/Step1_UbD.pdf.

Pitts, Joelle, Holger Lenz, and Marc Nash. 2013. "Lesson Plan Storyboard Template." Presentation at the New Literacies Alliance Quarterly Meeting.

Stiehl, Ruth, and Les Lewchuk. 2008. *The Outcomes Primer: Reconstructing the College Curriculum.* 3rd ed. Corvallis, OR: Learning Organization.

United States Geological Survey. 1998. "Bloom's Taxonomy of Questions Worksheet." https://pubs.usgs.gov/of/1998/of98-805/lessons/chpt4/taxon.htm.

Van Doren, Mark. 1943. *Liberal Education.* New York: Henry Holt and Company.

Vukas, Rachel, and Heather Collins. 2016. "Health Information Literacy Competencies: Curriculum Map." Unpublished manuscript. Kansas City, KS: The University of Kansas Medical Center.

The Design Process

4

In This Chapter

✓ Collaboration and Consistency

✓ Choosing an Instructional Design Model

✓ Rapid Prototyping in a Collaborative Environment

✓ The Design Process in Practice

TERMS

Assessments   Questions or interactive activities embedded in learning objects that are used to assess a student's understanding of concepts explored in the learning object.

Institution-agnostic content   Content created without institutional branding or identifying features so as to be reused or shared across multiple institutions.

Universal design   A set of principles for curriculum development that gives all individuals equal opportunities to learn (National Center on Universal Design for Learning 2014).

CHECKLIST

☐ Choose a developmental model.

☐ Create a style guide.

☐ Determine testing and reporting procedures.

☐ Determine learning object review process.

☐ Submit IRB (institutional review board) applications for testing.

One could describe design as a plan for arranging elements to accomplish a particular purpose.

—Charles Eames (1972)

This chapter builds on the learning design foundations laid in chapter 3 and offers several logistical considerations for the collaborative development of learning objects for library instruction. Starting with the tools and techniques to ensure consistency and accessibility in your learning objects, this chapter will walk you through the steps of learning object design and development. Instructional design models are discussed, including an in-depth treatment of the rapid prototyping model used by NLA instructional designers. The chapter concludes with considerations about learning object testing and review.

Collaboration and Consistency

Collaborative design projects can be difficult to manage, especially if multiple learning objects are being created by several individuals from many different institutions. It is important to create templates, guides, and other documentation to ensure the learning objects are consistent in terms of style and functionality.

Style Guide

The first step in this process is the creation of a style guide that content creators and instructional designers can use to manage the look and feel of the individual learning objects. Style guides come in all shapes and sizes. A simple Google search for "style guide" yields thousands of examples. But some components, outlined in this section, are essential to include in your style guide to ensure your collaborative design effort results in the most consistent and user-friendly learning objects.

Learning Object Content

- What each learning object should include (e.g., video, activity, assessments)
- The maximum amount of time each learning object should take students to finish
- How many and what type of assessments should be included in each learning object

Learning Object Structure

- Layout of individual pages or sections
- Navigation elements (e.g., top or side navigation, link structure, etc.)
- Page/element dimensions, particularly with mobile interfaces in mind

File Creation, Editing, and Management

- File storage and sharing
- File-naming protocols
- Citation/writing style

Branding and Identity

- Colors, including hex and RGB codes
- Fonts
- Logo
- Naming
- Copyright and licensing

Accessibility

- Checklist
- Section 508 guidelines (Section 508 Accessibility Program 2017)

FIGURE 4.1

Style Guide Excerpt: Branding and Identity

Colors

To maintain consistency across content, each text and element within the learning object will utilize the following colors:

Banner Text (gray): 44405f

Banner (white): ecebcd

Navigation Text (white): ffffff

Navigation Bar (gray): 72717a

Headings (gray): 4f4e5d

Links (green): 21877d

Links Hover (blue): 2880b5

Text (gray): 4f4e5d

Page (white): ffffff

Sidebar Text (green): 166a61

Sidebar (light blue): aac6c3

Footer Text (white): ffffff

Footer (off white): d9dbdc

Page Background Color (off white): d9dbdc

Fonts

In addition, font styles and sizes will be as follows:

Body Text: Arial 12 or 14

Headings: Arial 18, bold, 4f4e5d

Subhead 1: Arial 15, bold, 44a69c

Subhead 2: Arial 12 or 14, bold, 828191

Logo

These are the dimensions for the logo:

Width: 193 pixels

Height: 93 pixels

The NLA style guide was created shortly after the project began and included input from graphic designers at both founding institutions. Because each learning object is meant to be institution-agnostic, our graphic designers created a color palette and logo independent of partner institution colors and mascots. We branded the project as the New Literacies Alliance early on and determined that the content would be licensed through Creative Commons so that future partners could use and remix the learning objects as needed. We also decided that all learning objects would be built using SoftChalk software, so our style guide (see excerpt in figure 4.1) included color and font specifications for all of the structural elements within that system. The original NLA style guide has been a go-to resource for designers and developers in terms of font, color, and accessibility.

When creating your style guide, ensure all partner institutions are able to comply with the outlined style and accessibility standards. Use the principles of universal design for learning to ensure the highest number of partner institutions will be able to comply with your guidelines. The website and publications of the National Center on Universal Design for Learning (www.udlcenter.org) are good sources for information on this subject.

Development Guidelines

Collaborative design projects benefit from development or adaptation guidelines that articulate how each learning object is constructed, developed, and tested before being released to the public. These guidelines are particularly helpful for librarians who may not have instructional design or online learning object development experience.

There are few examples of instructional development guidelines on the Web, especially for collaborative projects. This is largely because each process will be determined by the instructional designers involved with the project, the chosen design model, and the composition of the design teams. What works for one project might not work for others, depending on a multitude of conditions and timelines. The following list presents the sections of the NLA development guidelines along with a brief description of each section's contents:

Design model   Articulates which instructional design model the collaboration will use to design and develop learning objects.

Storyboard and brainstorming   Describes how content creators and instructional designers work together to brainstorm learning outcomes and content into early storyboards.

Creating learning activities   Outlines the process for developing activities and assessments based on the learning outcome; includes a list of possible activities.

Learning object design and structure   Describes how the storyboard and activities will be adapted to SoftChalk using the chosen design model; includes the process of feedback and revision with content creators and instructional designers.

Content development   Describes how the content language, videos, images, and other materials will be fleshed out and finalized, including feedback and revision with content creators and instructional designers.

Testing, revision, and publishing   Articulates the process of learning object testing and reporting for final review and publishing.

The NLA adaptation guidelines have been re-envisioned over the life of the project, especially following the shift from an ADDIE-based design model to a rapid prototyping model (see following section), but the basic elements of the guidelines are still helpful, especially for new project participants.

Choosing an Instructional Design Model

Our purpose as creators of library instruction is to help our students and patrons become information literate, one learning outcome at a time. There are various instructional design approaches and models from which to choose to pursue this purpose. Numerous books have been written about the instructional design process in and out of library environments.

Many models are based on the ADDIE framework for instructional design: Analysis, Design, Development, Implementation, and Evaluation. Although many instructional design practitioners use ADDIE as a prescriptive model for developing instruction, it is actually a means of describing the essential components of any instructional design model (Brown and Green 2011). First envisioned and graphically represented in the early 1970s at Florida State University, the ADDIE framework began as a linear model for a designer to follow, working through each phase in the process to completion, starting with Analysis and ending with Evaluation. This is also called a waterfall approach (see figure 4.2), wherein each phase produces an end product that serves as the foundation for the next phase.

Designers since have realized the flaws in a linear design and production process and have adapted the ADDIE model to be more dynamic, at the very least incorporating some kind of evaluation during each phase (see figure 4.3).

Two examples of instructional design models that operate through the lens of the ADDIE model are Dick, Carey, and Carey's (2009) Systems Approach and Morrison, Ross, Kalman, and Kemp's (2012) Instructional Design Plan. Each plan offers a pathway from an idea for instructional

FIGURE 4.2

Waterfall Model

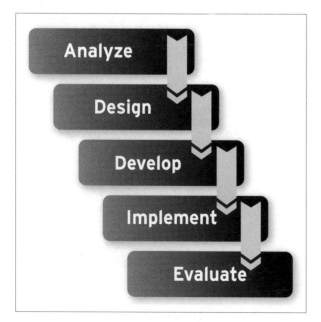

FIGURE 4.3

Modified ADDIE Model

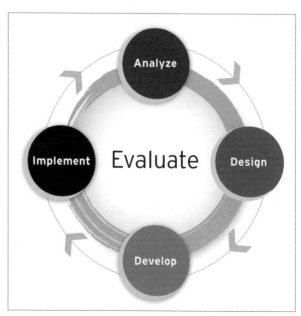

content based on demonstrated learning gaps to a learning object or environment that measures a learner's mastery of the gap area. ADDIE models are typically very time-intensive and focus much effort on early needs and learning analyses. Bell and Shank (2007) devote a chapter to ADDIE in their seminal work, *Academic Librarianship by Design: A Blended Librarian's Guide to the Tools and Techniques.* They note, however, that "[f]ew academic librarians have the necessary time to thoroughly and thoughtfully implement ADDIE in designing information literacy instruction" (43). If you have the time, the staff, and the means to design using ADDIE-framed models, they can offer a high level of detail, discipline, and up-front data to a project. Alternative design models exist, however, and can be implemented successfully in collaborative projects.

One such alternative, rapid prototyping, hails from the agile or iterative design model group. Rapid prototyping is similar in nature to some of the more recent evolutions of ADDIE, but this model comes to us from the software engineering world and has been adapted to educational design. The essential premise of rapid prototyping is the development of learning objects through a continuous design-evaluation cycle. Each iteration is tested with a sample of the target population and feedback is incorporated into the learning object design until a final product is achieved and implemented. The main difference between the ADDIE and rapid prototyping models is that the design and development phases happen independently in the ADDIE model and in tandem in the rapid prototyping model. The rapid prototyping model (see figure 4.4) also emphasizes reusing existing content rather than building every element from scratch.

FIGURE 4.4

Simplified Graphical Flowchart of the Rapid Prototyping Model

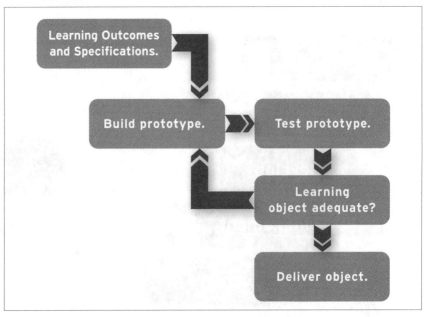

SOURCE: Modified from RMIT University 2017, figure 4, "Rapid Prototyping."

This kind of iterative design process can help a small design group get a better handle on what will be meaningful to student audiences within the context of draft content. Brown and Green (2011) describe rapid prototyping as a more constructive (as opposed to objective) approach to the problem by incorporating more opportunities for everyone involved in an instructional design project to participate in evaluating, problem solving, and revising. You can also use the rapid prototyping model to reduce risk during your design process. Through multiple tests with end users, you can identify the major design flaws, sticking points, and other problems before you put the learning object into production, saving your design group and your organization time and resources.

There are several ways to approach prototyping to determine which areas of your learning object to focus on and to give you an idea about the level of investment required for early prototypes.

Fidelity

Prototypes can be created using a range of fidelity options. You can start with something simple and of low fidelity, like a sketch or a storyboard on paper, and move toward high-fidelity prototypes (see figure 4.5) that incorporate polished videos and functional assessments or that are close to final production.

Vertical versus Horizontal Prototypes

Building vertical or horizontal prototypes during the development and testing of each learning object allows you to get a feel for how your audience will react to specific elements in the prototype or to the prototype in general (see figure 4.6).

> **Vertical prototypes** demonstrate the full functionality of a particular feature, such as a video or assessment question. Example:

FIGURE 4.5

Prototype Fidelity

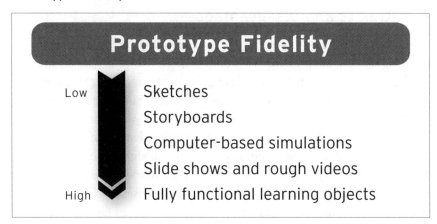

FIGURE 4.6

Scenario Prototype

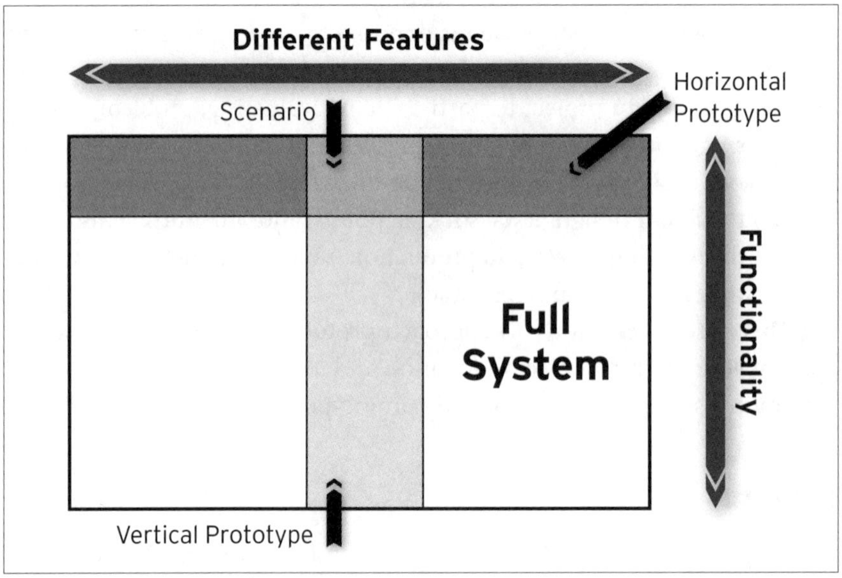

SOURCE: Nielsen, 1994, figure 1.

a working multiple choice question with near-final language and instructions.

Horizontal prototypes demonstrate the interface or learning object shell and usually just hint at the locations or functionality of the various features. Example: a mockup of the lesson interface without working links or navigation and using placeholders for various features.

The point at which vertical and horizontal prototypes converge is often a good point to conduct testing with your target audience. Provide a scenario in which they interact with a fully functional element within a mockup of the learning object. The feedback you receive allows you to expand on both vertical and horizontal elements toward a complete system.

Constraints and Disadvantages

Rapid prototyping is most effective for designing online asynchronous learning objects, such as videos or tutorials. This does not mean that the model cannot be applied to synchronous or in-person teaching environments, just that other instructional design models might be more efficient in those cases. There are also some potential disadvantages to this model to consider when choosing an approach, namely that it can be construed as undisciplined and informal. Instructional design experts Tripp and Bichelmeyer (1990) propose that there is also a tendency to get stuck in a design-by-repair rut, whereby your design team focuses less on the up-front brainstorming and careful design of learning content in favor of using the test feedback to drive design. It is also easy to skip important design steps in this model because of the rapid pace of design and development.

Rapid Prototyping in a Collaborative Environment

The rapid prototyping model is intense and can be difficult to manage under normal circumstances in a library instruction environment. These characteristics are amplified when using this model to design learning objects collaboratively. However, it is an especially useful tool when designing asynchronous learning objects among interinstitutional teams. This section highlights some of the rationale behind using this model for collaborative design, the various logistical considerations to think about ahead of your design project, and the importance of conducting a final review.

Rationale

Rapid prototyping can be an ideal design model for collaborative teams due to its informal nature. End users from different institutions and disciplines test learning objects during the rapid prototyping process. This process requires flexibility on the part of the content creation teams. If gaps are identified in the outcome or content or if the content is found to be somehow misaligned with student needs, the content creation process is revisited.

Prototype tests can (and should) be conducted at multiple locations, drawing feedback from multiple end user groups. This results in increased partner buy-in, design burden sharing, and also more robust feedback that can help design teams create content that will be more universally meaningful to students.

Logistics

When using rapid prototyping for instructional design, the following are important to consider and plan for, especially in an interinstitutional environment.

File Management

The rapid prototyping process results in many versions of learning objects files, from draft video scripts to graphic elements to edited text. If you are sharing the design process among two or more individuals, keep these files organized and labeled throughout the design process as well as after the learning object is implemented so it is easy to find files and make edits during routine maintenance.

- Store everything in one place.
- Use an agreed-upon naming convention.

- Create a usable hierarchy of files.
- Delete or archive old versions.
- File versions immediately or create an "inbox" within your hierarchy.
- Create shortcuts and back up your files often.

The NLA steering committee learned that project documentation could quickly become unwieldy and confusing. Elements of the project are currently stored in several locations, but most documents are housed in a Google collection that is accessible to all project members and periodically organized and cleaned out.

Testing

Target audience testing is an important aspect of rapid prototyping and one that you should plan for in advance. Ask yourself or your design team what you want to know about your learning object. Do you want to know what students think about the video or graphic you created? Can they pass the assessments at a certain level? Do you want to know their perceived level of confidence in understanding the content, or would you rather know what they believe could improve the lesson? Craft your questions around what you want to know, but keep the test as short as possible.

The next step is to schedule the tests and recruit students to participate (see figure 4.7). Determine ahead of time where the tests will take place and under what conditions. Finding test subjects can be easier said than done, especially at certain times of the year. For instance, the summer months and the three weeks around semester finals can be particularly tough times to find willing participants. Library student workers are often go-to test subjects, but take care to choose subjects without formal training in information literacy in order to get an unbiased result. Guerilla testing, when you

TESTING STEPS

1. Craft test questions—what do you want to know?
2. Get human subjects testing (IRB) approval, if publishing results.
3. Schedule tests.
4. Recruit test subjects.
5. Conduct test—record screen movements and answers to test questions.
6. Code and report on the results.
7. Use the results to improve your learning object.

FIGURE 4.7

NLA Testing Cycle

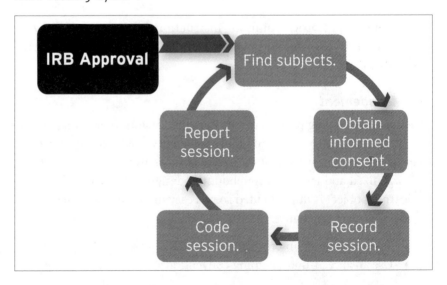

approach people to ask if they will participate in testing right now, can be a fun, albeit unpredictable, way to find test subjects. It usually works only if you can offer some kind of reward or goodie to entice them.

Institutional Review Boards (IRBs)

One of the first considerations is whether or not you plan to publish or otherwise release the results of your tests. If you do, most campuses in the United States and Canada have a research compliance office that can help you navigate the intricacies of human subjects testing. If you plan on administering the tests on multiple campuses, you will likely need to have a collaborator agreement on file with the compliance office for the lead investigator. If you do not plan on publishing or releasing the results in any way, you can forgo this step and focus on crafting your test questions.

Navigating the IRB at your institution can be tricky, but by starting early and asking questions, you will be able to create an application for human subjects testing that, once approved or determined to be exempt from review, will allow you to broadly publish the results. The first step in IRB approval is likely to be completion of training activities for anyone who will be involved in the testing process. You will then need to write a report on the research project, the subjects you intend to test, and the questions you will ask. The time it takes to submit your application and get approval or an exemption will vary depending on the institution and the policies in place, so plan several weeks or even months in advance, especially if you will have individuals from multiple institutions involved in the process.

Reporting

The NLA instructional designers record and code all tests conducted on each lesson in order to prepare reports for the small groups and the larger working group. Some team members like to watch the video recordings to see the nuanced answers and interactions with students. Whether you choose to make the recordings and reports available is up to you, but archive whatever documentation you create, especially if you need to return to the documents later to verify assumptions or answer questions.

Review

After weeks or months of content design and development, getting close to the release of a learning object can be exciting and exhausting. It is very tempting to skip a final thorough review of a lesson after you have spent so much time with it. But a final review is critical to the design process, in large part *because* you have spent so much time with the object. Fresh eyes can see things you may have missed in the minutiae. Final reviews should cover at least three main areas, not including the prior usability testing you conducted with students:

- Accessibility
- Copy editing
- Content peer review

TESTING BEST PRACTICES

How you structure your testing process will depend on how many team members you have and whether you plan to publish the results of your tests. The following are some best practices to keep in mind throughout the process.

- Pick a firm deadline for reporting out the results and stick to it. Tell everyone.
- Reuse as much content as you can: videos, parts of videos, scripts, graphics, LibGuides, etc.
- Submit an initial IRB application early. Once in the system, it takes less time to modify, if needed.
- Don't spend tons of time on the first prototype or testing. Get something up, and get some initial reactions. Look for big problems and deal-breakers early on; focus on finesse later.
- Don't fall in love with early content—it's going to change, especially after students test it.
- Keep files highly organized.
- Accept imperfection—it will never be perfect.

An accessibility check can be tedious. Tabbing through every element on your keyboard and rereading video transcripts are not particularly exciting tasks. But these checks often uncover content that is largely inaccessible to someone using screen readers or keyboard navigation to interact with your content. Ensure your content is, at the very least, compliant with Section 508 of the Web accessibility standards outlined by the federal government (Section 508 Accessibility Program 2017). Consider working with your campus accessibility office to ensure compliance with college or university accessibility standards.

Copy editing is something to outsource beyond your immediate design team. Ask a colleague or even a student from the English department to read your content with a critical eye, following the writing style requirements outlined in your style guide. It is very likely that this person will find errors that your eyes skipped over during multiple readings of the content.

Finally, ask a colleague outside of the design team to peer review the content of the lesson. Ask this person to consider if the content is accurate, clear, and fully representative of the library or information literacy issue you are trying to teach. You could even create an external review group within your collaboration that would be responsible for conducting reviews as lessons are developed.

The Design Process in Practice

The NLA working group spent considerable time perfecting a design process that worked efficiently for partners across several institutions and time zones. We started on a style guide early in the project, which was a boon to our future design teams, who were able to easily begin creating content within the style parameters already in place and vetted through graphic designers at multiple institutions. We created a template design within SoftChalk that adhered to the style parameters and could be easily applied to any new lessons. Content adaptation guidelines were developed as we worked through content design and development for several lessons. We learned what worked and did not work for our team members and created documentation to match.

One hard lesson we learned after bringing a new partner on board is that technical design guidelines, style guides, and other documentation can be intimidating to new project members, especially those who are new to both interinstitutional collaboration and online instructional design. We have since significantly pared down the documentation that new partners are given. Instead, we work more individually with them in design team settings so they can observe before contributing fully to content creation, joining in only after they feel comfortable with the process. We have instituted a similar process for new instructional designers on the project. They observe and help with design elements over the course of a learning object and take on leadership for learning object development when they feel comfortable with the model.

We started with a modified ADDIE model during the early stages of the collaboration. Once we learned that the student testing feedback was invaluable to the final design of most lessons, we incorporated routine testing into the process in spring 2015 using the rapid prototyping model. The typical cycle of development is an initial long brainstorming session and subsequent meetings resulting in an early prototype. The instructional designers test the prototype with two or three library student workers who are able to fill in the gaps in the early content with their existing library experience. That feedback is used to revise the lesson into a second prototype that is tested with a nonlibrary student group or, at the very least, a group of library students who do not work at the reference desk or on projects related to information literacy instruction. That feedback is incorporated into a semifinal or final prototype that includes videos, draft images, and other elements in their semifinal forms. This prototype is usually tested with a group of nonlibrary student volunteers who answer calls for research participation or who are encouraged by faculty teaching their courses. Their feedback is incorporated into a final version of the learning object that goes through an accessibility and copyright check before a final review by the larger working group. The rapid prototyping process looks similar to that shown in figure 4.8 for the NLA project.

FIGURE 4.8

NLA Rapid Prototyping Process

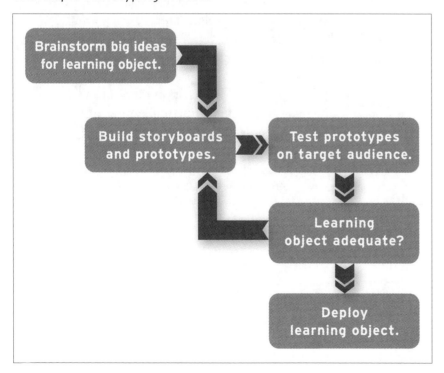

This process, while intensive, allows us to move quickly through the stages of design using data-driven iterations. We avoid the circular speculation about student response and learning that we sometimes see with collaborative instructional design projects.

Of course, not every learning object and design team are the same. Occasionally, lesson development is extended to account for the nature of the content being developed and the feedback we get from student testers. For example, our "Scholarly Conversations" lesson took almost a full calendar year to create. The *Framework for Information Literacy for Higher Education* (ACRL 2016) provided a lens for scholarship as a conversation for the first time and members of the team struggled to place their teaching experiences and needs in that context. Several months into the design process, the team realized that the content they had created did not clearly address one outcome but was scattered among several competing ideas. Seeing the disparity in assessments and activities forced the team to reset, come to a consensus, and develop content that was still relatively new to them in terms of instructional experience. The result was a highly visual and unique lesson that many students have indicated is engaging and valuable. This lesson has been accepted in the PRIMO peer-reviewed instructional content database.

CRITICAL QUESTIONS

1. What instructional development model will work best for your team?
2. How many learning objects can you reasonably complete per year with your current project staff and using your chosen development model?
3. What style parameters are critical to the success and branding of your project?
4. Do you plan to publish the results of your project and, specifically, the results of student/patron testing?
5. How will you test your learning objects, including recruiting students/patrons?
6. What will your final reviews consist of and whom will you ask to help with each aspect?

References

ACRL (Association of College & Research Libraries). 2016. *Framework for Information Literacy for Higher Education.* Chicago: American Library Association. www.ala.org/acrl/standards/ilframework.

Bell, Steven J., and John Shank. 2007. *Academic Librarianship by Design: A Blended Librarian's Guide to the Tools and Techniques.* Chicago: American Library Association.

Brown, Abbie, and Timothy D. Green. 2011. *The Essentials of Instructional Design: Connecting Fundamental Principles with Process and Practice.* Boston: Pearson Education.

Dick, Walter, Lou Carey, and James O. Carey. 2009. *The Systematic Design of Instruction.* 7th ed. New York: Merrill/Pearson.

Eames, Charles, with Madame L. Amic. 1972. "Design Q&A Text." Eames Office. Accessed March 31, 2017. www.eamesoffice.com/the-work/design-q-a-text.

Morrison, Gary R., Steven M. Ross, Howard K. Kalman, and Jerrold E. Kemp. 2012. *Designing Effective Instruction.* 7th ed. Hoboken, NJ: John Wiley and Sons.

National Center on Universal Design for Learning. 2014. "What Is UDL?" Last updated July 31. www.udlcenter.org/aboutudl/whatisudl.

Nielsen, Jakob. 1994. "Guerrilla HCI: Using Discount Usability Engineering to Penetrate the Intimidation Barrier." Nielson Norman Group, January 1. www.nngroup.com/articles/guerrilla-hci.

RMIT University. 2017. "Plan Website Development." Accessed March 7. www.dlsweb.rmit.edu.au/toolbox/ecommerce/ddw_respak/ddw_e1/html/ddw_e1_plan.htm.

Section 508 Accessibility Program. 2017. "Section 508 Law and Related Laws and Policies." Accessed March 29. https://section508.gov/content/learn/laws-and-policies.

Tripp, Steven D., and Barbara Bichelmeyer. 1990. "Rapid Prototyping: An Alternative Instructional Design Strategy." *Educational Technology Research and Development* 38 (1): 31–44.

Implementation

In This Chapter

✓ Laying the Groundwork

✓ Soft Launch

✓ Wider Implementation

✓ Implementation in Practice

Everything is impossible until it is done.

—Robert Goddard (1921)

This chapter discusses moving learning objects from the design and development stages to implementing them in a learning environment. While implementation may seem like the culmination of all of your other work, you should read this chapter even as you are creating the learning objects and figuring out the technology.

Laying the Groundwork

Whether you are planning a simple or complex implementation, policies, procedures, deadlines, and workflows can impact your project. Laying the groundwork means that you are not only aware of the need for but are prepared to carry out these tasks:

- Obtaining permissions
- Establishing and meeting deadlines
- Managing records
- Identifying and contacting partners

Because this is a collaboration, you should expect differences between institutions, whether in procedures for approving academic requirements, concerns about data sharing, or the academic calendar. You will need to lay the groundwork to the best of your ability at each institution. Even if one institution is providing project leadership, do not focus solely on that institution's procedures. Other institutions may still have concerns or requirements that will impact your implementation. Doing your due diligence ensures that there will be fewer roadblocks.

Start laying the groundwork as soon as you can; do not wait until the learning objects are almost complete. Requirements for approval, deadlines, and data-sharing agreements may impact how you design learning objects or the technology you use. Additionally, meeting some institutional requirements may necessitate lead times of a semester or more. Depending upon the level at which you are implementing your learning objects, you may need to leverage the support of your dean and/or director, so be sure to keep the appropriate people apprised of your progress.

Document your groundwork, preferably so that your collaborators can also access the information. This documentation not only supports project management but also becomes invaluable in the face of the inevitable turnover of individual collaborators. With the NLA, we relied on a shared Google Docs folder, but you may find formal project management and collaboration sites more useful for your project.

Obtaining Permissions

Will you need official approval to implement your project? Who grants this approval? These two questions serve as your starting point for obtaining permissions. Whether you are working toward making the learning objects a requirement for any group of students will also influence the kind of permissions you will need. At the simplest end of the spectrum, learning objects that are used on an à la carte basis—for example, embedded in a research guide—may require no permissions at all. At the other end, establishing the learning objects as a requirement for enrollment or graduation may necessitate a series of permissions from the department level up to institutional governing bodies. Universities vary in institutional culture, practices, and mandated procedures, making it difficult to describe all routes to take to obtain permissions. Fortunately, the following experts and resources already on your campus can provide you with enough information to get started:

- Departmental curriculum committees
- Faculty academic affairs committees
- Registrar's office
- Policy and procedures manuals or university handbooks
- Library dean/director

Many of these resources focus on credit-bearing classes or programs. When implementing learning objects outside of this realm, look for existing programs as models. For instance, an increasing number of universities require incoming students to complete online training programs like alcohol awareness, sexual assault prevention, or IT security. When trying to add learning objects as a module in a cornerstone or capstone course, or in other existing courses, investigate how programs normally update their course content. While some course changes occur to meet accreditation requirements and are more or less mandated, other programs invariably update to improve the success of their graduates. Ascertaining how these changes are instituted may provide a path to implementing learning objects.

While collaborations can seem cumbersome when faced with obtaining approval from so many different institutions, collaborations also offer resources and reinforcement. At the most basic level, reuse content in your application materials. As more collaborators obtain approval, indicate this in documentation submitted to institutions that are slower or more resistant. Seeing the approval from other institutions reinforces the legitimacy of the project. Another benefit of collaborations is that insights from a friend on an academic affairs committee at Institution A may help break through a barrier or misunderstanding at Institution B. Do not collaborate just on creating learning objects; collaborate on learning how to navigate your institutional requirements.

Do not overlook permissions or approval needed from within your own library. This might involve an administrative body signing off on the project, but it will always involve obtaining buy-in from colleagues. Communicate early and regularly with your colleagues, particularly if they will be expected or required to use the learning objects themselves.

Finally, be sure to keep your dean/director/sponsor apprised of your progress in obtaining permissions. When this person has the facts on hand, he or she can more effectively advocate for the project when questions arise.

Establishing and Meeting Deadlines and Timelines

The terms *deadlines* and *timelines* are often used interchangeably. We are defining *deadlines* as concrete dates and *timelines* as plans for how long it will take to accomplish something.

Deadlines can be established internally by the project team or externally by outside agencies. You will have more flexibility and control over the internal deadlines. Pertinent outside deadlines include these:

- Academic calendars
- Application/approval deadlines
- Fiscal year start and end dates
- Grant deadlines

Internal deadlines ensure that a project makes meaningful and timely progress. These deadlines might be aspirational (roll out three learning objects by start of the fall semester) or constructive, such as breaking up larger projects into smaller segments with specified due dates.

Timelines and deadlines are symbiotic. In some cases, timelines will determine your deadlines. For instance, if you know that it will take seven months to design a dashboard that will serve as the primary user interface, then you cannot have a deadline for going live until after that seven-month mark. Deadlines determine timelines in situations like this: you know that the learning objects need to be functioning by the spring semester, so the planning, design, and testing need to be accomplished before the first day of the spring semester.

When constructing timelines, be aware that, in our experience, most projects take one and a half to two times longer than expected. Be aspirational, but realistic. Take into account team members' workloads throughout the academic year. Within the NLA, we have found distinct differences between institutions in regard to busy times. We used a Doodle poll to ask members to indicate which months they could devote to the project, which months they could if needed, and which months they could not. This created a quick visualization of the year that we can use in long-term planning. Knowing that members of your team are unavailable to work on the learning objects at certain times of the year helps establish reasonable timelines and deadlines.

However deadlines and timelines are established, they are vital for keeping a project moving forward. Centrally record deadlines from all institutions so that all members of the project can readily contextualize when things need to happen. A project manager monitors deadlines and helps the team establish timelines to ensure deadlines are met. If a project manager is not available, tools like Gantt charts or even well-maintained calendars can still help with meeting deadlines. It is very easy for project members to prioritize other work over the collaboration's work without concrete goals

FIGURE 5.1

NLA Deliverable Schedule

Deliverable	Deadline	Roles
Glossary of terms (objective versus outcome, etc.)	November 1st	Anne, Heather, Joelle, Sara
Style guide: guidelines for accessibility, navigation, design, etc.	November 1st	Joelle, Holger, Marc
Lesson plan template	November 1st	Anne, Heather, Joelle, Sara
Guidelines on how to write outcomes and lessons	November 16th	Anne, Heather, Joelle, Sara
Adaptation guidelines for content creators to work with instructional designers	December 14th	Holger, Marc, Joelle

and timelines. Deadlines and timelines also ensure accountability to your project sponsors. Periodically revisit your timelines and deadlines in light of your goals and progress. Figure 5.1 outlines the deliverables, deadlines, and those responsible for meeting the deadlines during a particular time frame.

Managing Records

The learning objects will likely generate records related to their use and completion, from basic use statistics to student scores or grades. Develop a system to track, collect, organize, or disseminate this information. Review what information is confidential or has constraints about what can be shared, particularly in regard to the Family Educational Rights and Privacy Act (FERPA; US Department of Education, 2015). Contact your university's counsel, registrar's office, or other appropriate office to ascertain how student scores/records should be handled.

To develop a records management system appropriate for your project, consider the following questions:

1. What types of data are being collected?
   - Scores
   - Student responses (short answer or other qualitative data)
   - Student identifiers (name, student ID numbers, other demographics)
   - Learning object data (times accessed, completion time)
   - IP (Internet protocol) addresses of users
2. What will you do with the information?
   - Assess the learning objects.
   - Track which courses used the learning objects.
   - Provide a grade or certificate of completion.
3. Who needs access to the information?
   - Students
   - Librarians working with classes
   - Course instructors
   - Registrar's office
   - Members of the project team
4. What institutional guidelines or regulations constrain use and access to the learning objects?
   - FERPA
   - Status of librarians as faculty (may limit rights to access student records)
5. Where will the information be stored?
   - Secure server hosted by one institution
   - The cloud
   - Shared network/server that can be accessed by some or all project members
   - University student information systems

6. How will the records be accessed, disseminated, and reported?
   - Self-service
   - Requested from hosting institution
   - Automatic reporting
   - Student transcripts

Managing data and records can raise many questions before reaching resolution. Start this process well before going live with the learning objects. As with other aspects of the project, centrally document decisions and include contact information (names, offices, etc.) of those you consulted.

Identifying and Contacting Partners

Whom do you need to work with outside the project team in order to implement the learning objects? Identify partners by determining the following:

- Who will help obtain permissions.
- Who can advocate for the learning objects.
- What classes or programs will be targeted for the soft launch and wider implementation.
- Which librarians or library staff will use the learning objects.

Potential partners include the following:

- Institutional academic directors: provost, director of first-year programs, deans, department heads, directors of undergraduate or graduate studies.
- Course collaborators/teaching partners: faculty, instructors, teaching assistants.
- Academic affairs personnel: college/department curriculum committees, faculty senators, registrar's office, graduate school administrators.
- Library collaborators: instruction librarians, reference librarians, peer mentors.
- Advocates: university library committee, student ambassador groups, advisors.

When identifying partners, consider those with whom you already have a good working relationship. Seek out people who have experience with approval processes. For instance, professional staff in departmental offices or the registrar's office handle the day-to-day logistics of many university processes. Other good partners include the faculty member who has served on a committee for umpteen years and knows the politics intimately or the graduate teaching assistants who teach multiple sections of composition.

Reach out to partners well ahead of deadlines. Find out if they have scheduling conflicts (e.g., going on sabbatical) or concerns (e.g., how the scores from learning objects will be recorded and shared). Consider the multiple roles your partners will play when you design your marketing materials. Some will need to understand the vision, others the pedagogy, and still others the actual logistics of using the learning objects.

Soft Launch

Chapter 4 described rapid prototyping as a way to iteratively test learning objects during their creation. Now, you need to conduct a soft launch before rolling out the learning objects to all of your constituents. A soft launch allows you to conduct a controlled rollout of the learning objects with a small cohort in order to troubleshoot, test functionality and workflows, and assess the pedagogy of the learning objects in a real-world environment.

Pick your soft launch partners carefully. Faculty, or programs, with whom you are comfortable working make good teaching partners because you already know how to work together. Identify teaching partners who understand that they are helping test the learning objects, who can adjust their syllabi or lesson plans if the learning objects do not work, and who will provide honest feedback. It is just as important to identify members of your team who demonstrate the same qualities and who are receptive to feedback for the soft launch. You are testing the learning objects, and there will be problems. Be sure that the members of your team who are participating in the soft launch are comfortable getting negative feedback and respond well to uncertainty.

Conduct the soft launch at multiple institutions. One of the benefits of an interinstitutional collaboration is the variety of environments in which to test the learning objects. Additionally, the unique blend of technologies, policies, and partners at each institution means that you cannot rely on the outcomes of a soft launch at only one institution. Testing the learning objects at multiple institutions highlights those issues which are specific to an institution (firewalls) or a learning management system (incompatible software) and those which are more universal.

Test the learning objects through the entire workflow, from the starting point when students encounter the learning objects through the final point of data collection and reporting. You may find it is more practical to conduct several tests or soft rollouts at different stages of the workflow. This can increase the time it will take to achieve the complete rollout of the project but does recognize that your team can monitor and fix only so much at a time.

Be prepared for the soft launch to generate a flurry of troubleshooting and fixes. This is exactly what you want. It is easier, both logistically and politically, to successfully roll out a project if you have encountered and addressed most of the problems first. This also offers you the confidence to respond to the inevitable questions about how it will work.

Use the soft launch to test the following project parameters:

1. Communication with teaching partners
    *   Can you concisely explain the value of the learning objects?
    *   Do your partners have questions that you cannot answer?

2. Lead time
    *   How much lead time do your teaching partners need to integrate learning objects into their classes?
    *   Does the librarian or project team need any lead time to make the learning objects available for a particular class or student?

3. Embedding learning objects
    *   Who can embed the learning objects into a course or learning management system (LMS)?
    *   How extensive does training need to be for the person embedding the learning objects?
    *   Can the learning objects be used in LMSs or on websites at all partner institutions?

4. Student access to and completion of learning objects
    *   How do students know they need to complete the learning objects?
    *   Do students need instructions to complete the learning objects apart from any guidance offered in the learning objects?
    *   How do students know they have successfully completed the learning objects?
    *   What happens if the learning objects do not work or students cannot complete the learning objects?

5. Recording, accessing, and reporting student scores
    *   How do you know if the students have completed the learning objects?
    *   How do the teaching partners know if students have completed the learning objects?
    *   Does the system capture enough information to appropriately assign credit?
    *   Can everyone who needs to access scores do so?

6. Troubleshooting
    *   Can users consistently access the learning objects?
    *   Who can fix problems?
    *   How are problems reported?
    *   How long does it take to get a response or fix?
    *   How frequently do issues arise?
    *   Do these issues raise an insurmountable barrier to rollout?

7. Assessment of the questions (see also chapter 7, "Assessment")
    *   Do questions in the learning objects assess student learning?

- Are there questions that students most commonly answer incorrectly?
- Are the questions too easy? Do all students answer all of the questions correctly?

8. Impact on library instruction
   - Are students learning the content to the extent that the librarian needs to change how he or she teaches the class?
   - Do the learning objects distract from library instruction, such as requiring extensive troubleshooting or necessitating clarification?

9. Accessibility
   - Are the learning objects accessible to all users regardless of device (computer or mobile device) or visual, hearing, learning, or other impairment?

10. Interinstitutional issues
    - Can all of the institutions access and use the learning objects?
    - Is content appropriate for partner institutions (e.g., degree of difficulty for the learning objects, learning object content that conforms with university standards, learning object content that is compatible with university culture)?

11. Workloads and workflows
    - Can your team handle the amount of work required to launch and support the learning objects?

However you collect or record the answers to these questions, use that information. It will allow you to do the following:

- Fix technical problems.
- Address communication issues.
- Develop FAQs for students, librarians, and teaching partners.
- Understand how the learning objects might affect your teaching/work with the class/program.
- Initially assess student learning.
- Collect anecdotes of success.
- Revise learning objects.

For instance, the NLA collected data on student responses to the questions embedded in the learning objects (see chapter 7, "Assessment," for more information). Based on an analysis of the student responses, an assessment team recommended edits to certain questions in order to alleviate confusion (see figure 5.2). These changes were reviewed and implemented before the wider rollout.

The soft launch also answered a key question: Would students translate concepts from the learning objects to their own work? While our content creators strove to create learning objects that would be relevant across disciplines, the learning objects never exactly match class assignments.

FIGURE 5.2

Assessment Group Recommendations

Four questions were identified as needing revision (see Word document for text of questions and answers*); the group's recommendations for revision are included as well:

a. Asking the Right Questions, question #1

 We recommend adding the word "people" after elderly.

b. Asking the Right Questions, question #2

 At this point, we are doing some checking on back-end issues and will recommend a format change for this question.

c. Asking the Right Questions, question #3

 We recommend changing the wording of the question to "Which question contains all 5Ws and is the most developed?"

d. Search Strategies, question #2

 In addition to reviewing its location within the tutorial (at the end versus earlier, adjacent to the information for it), we recommend a revision to lessen the confusion with regard to the all-caps H1N1, Boolean operators, parentheses, and quotation marks, as there is a lot going on and it runs together. To start, we would recommend removing the parentheses in the question itself and changing the wording to "also known as Swine Flu."

---

*The text of the original questions and answers follows:

1. Which 5W criteria would you add to the following question in order to narrow the scope of investigation? "Are flu rates higher among the elderly than in other populations in the past decade?"

 ☐ Who ☐ What ☐ Where ☐ When ☐ Why

2. Match the items. The task is to match the lettered items with the correct numbered items. Appearing below is a list of lettered items. Following that is a list of numbered items. Each numbered item is followed by a drop-down. Select the letter in the drop-down that best matches the numbered item with the lettered alternatives.

 a. A subject you are investigating.   1. Scope of Investigation

 b. How large or small your investigation will be.   2. Research Topic

 c. What drives your investigation. Something you want to explore and answer. 3. Research Question

3. Considering the 5Ws, which of the following research questions is most developed.

 a. What are the best practices in communicating about the flu vaccine?

 b. What are the current best practices in communicating with area at-risk urban families about the safety of the flu vaccine to encourage immunization?

 c. What are the best practices in communicating with area families about the safety of the flu vaccine to encourage immunization?

 d. What are the current best practices for communicating about the flu vaccine to encourage immunization and build trust for future conversations?

4. Which is the best-designed search string based on the following research question? "Did increased airport flu screening reduce the spread of the H1N1 (Swine Flu) in 2014?"

 a. (H1N1 OR "swine flu") AND "airport screen*" AND 2014

 b. airport screening AND H1N1 OR swine flu AND 2014

 c. airport screening AND swine flu OR airport flu screen* AND 2014

 d. screen* AND airport AND H1N1 OR 2014

Additionally, our decision to create database-agnostic learning objects (i.e., we created mocked-up search interfaces rather than using screenshots of specific databases) meant that students would encounter different interfaces in the real world. We learned that these decisions did not create a barrier to student learning. Specifically, the "Search Strategies" learning object has a storyline about searching for information about flu shots. All of the text, activities, and assessment questions relate to flu shots. One of the soft launch courses was a first-year history class researching early Western empires. Nonetheless, during the in-person library class, students readily applied the methods from the learning object to class activities. In fact, students jumped ahead of the librarian's expectations, and during a hands-on activity in JSTOR, they began shouting out the methods they used to change the number and type of search results they found. Had the soft launch revealed that students could not transfer the concepts, we would have had to revisit the learning object design. Instead, we were able to move ahead with the wider launch.

Wider Implementation

Once issues raised during the soft launch have been addressed, you are ready for a wider implementation. Wider implementation requires more than completed learning objects. Even if the project team members are the only ones using the learning objects, you will need to both market the learning objects and provide support for them. The wider implementation will undoubtedly involve more people than just those on the project team, and you will need to provide resources for fellow librarians, teaching partners, and students. In order to educate and support the expanded user base, develop materials in the following areas:

- Marketing
- Pedagogy
- Learning object access
- Technical support
- Assessment

Marketing

When initiating the wider implementation, be prepared to talk about the learning objects and your project a lot. *Field of Dreams* aside, if you build it, they do not automatically come. Marketing at this point has a high educational quotient. Your users need to know more than that the learning objects exist; you want them to learn to use them. This is when elevator speeches, flyers, a website, and compiled FAQs become particularly useful. Consistent and ongoing communication ensures that partners and students are aware of and understand the purpose of the learning objects.

When marketing, create effective messages by communicating how your project helps faculty and students do whatever they are doing, better. Potter (2012) notes that when we focus on the product or project, members of our audience find that it

> [p]uts the onus on them to think about how they integrate that content into their lives; many people simply don't have time to analyse what we're offering in that way. We should be showing them explicitly how we can help them so they need no imagination to understand it. (2)

That is, do not focus on *what* you created but on *why* someone would use it.

Develop different messages for different audiences to answer their specific information needs. Create a pool of content that can be repackaged for e-mails, websites, flyers, presentations, press releases, and other outlets. If you can, work with a professional graphic designer and/or writer. Such professionals are experienced in working with institutional communications and marketing offices, understand the nuances of designing and writing for print and the Web, and more accurately estimate marketing timelines and costs.

Essential marketing materials include these:

- Elevator speeches and talking points
- FAQs
- Regular reports

Elevator speeches and *talking points* are concise descriptions of your project. Use an elevator speech to briefly explain why someone would use your project and to entice that person into asking for more information. Develop several talking points that can stand alone or be mixed and matched in presentations, e-mails, or other communications. (See appendix F for the NLA talking points.)

FAQs answer logistical and pedagogical questions. Use FAQs to provide information about technology requirements, use with LMSs, pedagogy, and the myriad of questions that arose during the soft launch and wider implementation. Be sure to include contact information somewhere within the FAQs.

Regular reports provide users and stakeholders with updates on the project on a periodic basis. Reports can include how much the learning objects are used, what classes or institutions are using them, if new learning objects are coming, and if some learning objects have been retired or are being edited. Regular reports both share information about the impact of the project and let potential users and partners know that it is still a going concern.

Not everyone on the team will be a natural marketer. Additionally, librarians who are using the learning objects but are not on the team will rely heavily on these materials to introduce the learning objects into their outreach, instruction, and/or reference efforts. Even if the learning objects

---

NLA'S WHAT AND WHY

What Online asynchronous information literacy learning objects.

Why Ensure students have a common baseline understanding of finding, evaluating, sharing, and creating information that will allow a higher-level exploration of discipline- and course-specific information literacy concepts.

NLA ELEVATOR SPEECH

The New Literacies Alliance is a multi-institutional collaborative effort that creates and shares a broad range of online information literacy lessons. These ACRL (2016) *Framework*-based lessons can be embedded in websites and LibGuides and incorporated into most LMSs. Sharing is key to our mission, so each lesson features a Creative Commons BY-NC-SA (Attribution-NonCommercial-ShareAlike) License and our content is not tied to any one institution, so educators can use and adapt the material as they see fit.

will be used in a prescribed manner on campus, such as being an enroll-ment requirement, your partners inside and outside of the library will undoubtedly be called upon to explain the purpose of the learning objects. Colleagues are more likely to suggest using or to discuss the learning objects if they have marketing materials to fall back on.

Identify team members to proactively promote the learning objects. This promotion can include these approaches:

- Speaking at faculty or student orientations
- Presenting the learning objects at colleges, departments, or decision-making groups on campus, like faculty senate or cur-riculum committees
- Liaising between the project team members, librarians, and teaching partners
- Presenting at conferences
- Serving as contact persons for inquiries about the project
- Submitting updates to professional publications

Within the NLA, our steering committee typically serves in this role; we have been marketing the project both within our institutions and to the academic library world since we began. Our Deans and Directors Sponsors Group promotes the learning objects at various consortium meetings and to fellow deans and directors.

As noted earlier, expect to talk about the project a lot. How do you know when you have talked about the project enough? Your marketing plan can establish clear rubrics, with goals like recruiting X number of classes or speaking at specific orientations. Otherwise, aim for *saturation* and an *echo*. When you attend a faculty meeting and almost everyone nods instead of looking quizzical when you mention the project, you are reaching satura-tion. When you are regularly invited to "talk about that project," you are reaching saturation. When a department head shares in an accreditation meeting that the learning objects are scaffolded into a degree program, you are hearing an echo. When an instructor asks about using the learning objects after hearing about them from another professor, you are hearing an echo. When a library student ambassador suggests that all students should be required to complete learning objects like the ones she did for a public speaking library assignment (true story!), you are hearing an echo.

Hitting saturation and hearing an echo are not signals to stop marketing the learning objects. Instead, they indicate that it is time to shift to the next phase in your marketing plan. There will always be new faculty, librarians, and students. You may identify different target audiences, refresh materials to represent upgraded or new features, or highlight certain aspects of the learning objects, such as assessment results.

Members of K-State's NLA contingent talk about the project at least once a semester at the K-State Libraries' all-staff meeting, offering a report on the overall progress, highlighting use in particular classes, and dem-onstrating new features. We also report at least annually to the University

TIP **Saturation** is that point when people come to expect that you will talk about the learning objects; the fact that they exist is no longer new information to your audience. An **echo** is when people talk about learning objects without your having to lay the groundwork.

Library Committee (an advisory board comprised of faculty, staff, and students), the K-State Libraries' Strategic Leadership Council (the leadership team comprised of library administrators, including deans, associate deans, and department heads), the Libraries' Student Ambassadors, and to our Academic Services Department. With our wider implementation, we are pitching the learning objects at departmental meetings across campus as part of our liaison relationships.

Pedagogy

Whether the learning objects will be used in a prescribed manner or à la carte, develop guidance about why, how, and when to use the learning objects. Explain the theory or perspective that frames the learning objects. Describe the logistics so partners understand how to request the learning objects and obtain student scores. Offer examples of how the learning objects have been or could be packaged or integrated into courses or programs. Teaching faculty and fellow librarians are already working with their own student learning outcomes, so your material should help them understand how the learning objects will support those outcomes. (See chapter 3 for more information about mapping the learning objects and the ACRL *Framework* to curricula.)

The NLA developed content for an instructor's primer that can serve as a handout or reside on our website. The primer provides enough information for teaching partners to understand how the learning objects are intended to be used without overwhelming them with minutiae. The primer describes the following:

- The role librarians play in the instruction process
- When to contact librarians
- When the learning objects should ideally be integrated into a course
- Ways to use the learning objects in courses
- How the learning objects are scored
- How to identify relevant learning objects for a course
- Learning objects organized by themes

Learning Object Access

Ensure that your partners can find and play with learning objects, and make it easy to do so. Beyond developing an informational website or LibGuide for your learning objects, there are basic Web optimization techniques, like short URLs and Google keyword mapping, that simplify access.

The NLA initially housed information about our project on a K-State LibGuide. That guide explains the project, features versions of the learning objects that do not collect scores, and provides access to scorable versions of the learning objects. Some of our collaborating institutions created information on their own websites. This allows librarians to offer information

TIP **Short URLs** are easier to remember and key into an address bar. If you cannot create a short URL on your website, use URL shortening sites like Ow.ly and Bitly.com. The shortened URLs redirect users to the actual site. Another benefit of using a URL shortener is that you can customize the URL so it is recognizable as being related to your learning objects.

If your university or library website uses a search box, such as the Google search box, work with your Web developer/librarian to add **Google keyword mapping** for your project. Provide a list of terms that you anticipate will be used when searching your website for your project. These can include the project's name and/or acronym, language you use to describe the project in marketing materials, and how you have heard other people describe your project. These terms are mapped, or linked, to your project's webpage. With keyword mapping, your project will rise to the top of the search results list.

specific to their institutions' partners, such as contacts and instructions for using the learning objects in their LMSs.

Now that the project team is growing, we have moved the NLA to its own website: http://newliteraciesalliance.org. While it is still hosted by a partner institution (Oklahoma State University), the URL itself is branded to the NLA. By shifting to a new site, more partner institutions can access and update the website, which also increases collaborative opportunities.

Technical Support

Between establishing the technical parameters for the project (see chapter 6) and the soft launch, you should have a good idea of the kinds of technical support and troubleshooting needed. Ideally, colleagues from multiple institutions will be able to provide some level of support. Leverage the diversity of institutions in your collaboration to troubleshoot issues such as those related to particular LMSs or student information systems. Ensure that it is clear whom to contact for support. This may involve a shared e-mail, a Web submission form, or a phone number. Wider implementation entails providing support for more users. Closely monitor the impact on the workload of those providing support. Provide FAQs so users can get answers quickly. As you better understand tech support workflows, adjust your processes or even develop do-it-yourself options.

The NLA realized fairly quickly in our wider implementation that our system of providing links to learning objects and tracking their use took more time than anticipated. One of our instructional designers created a self-service request form using Google Docs to generate links for librarians or faculty (see figure 5.3). She also identified a way to use Google Analytics to track how many times learning objects are used. Both solutions required an up-front investment of time but automated two processes, saving time in the long term.

FIGURE 5.3

Self-Service Request for NLA Lessons

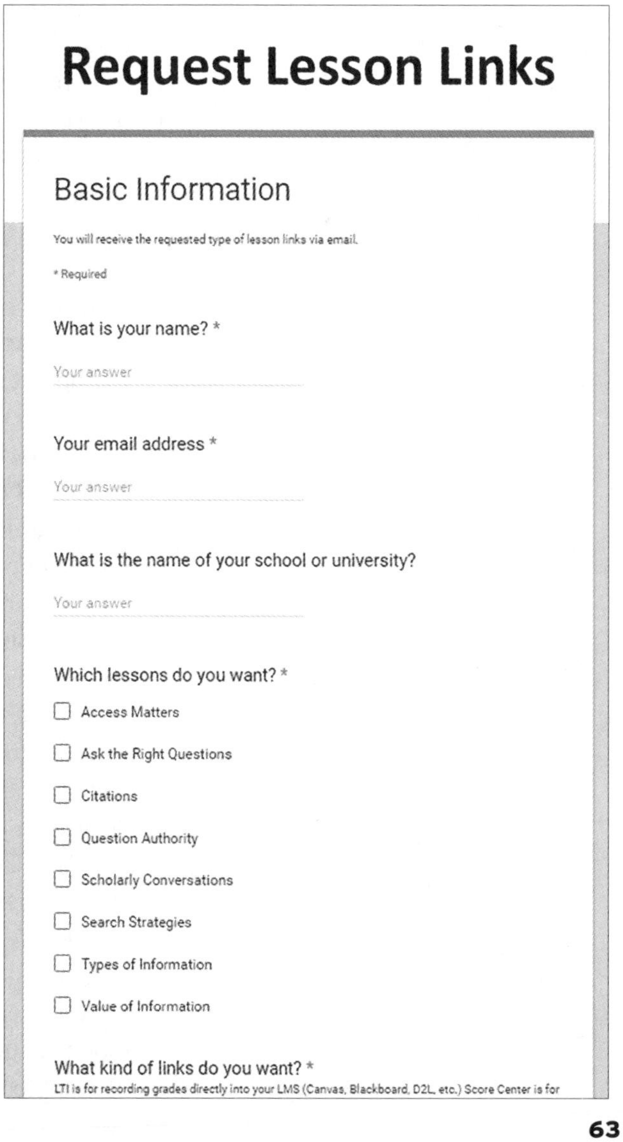
Request Lesson Links

Basic Information

You will receive the requested type of lesson links via email.

* Required

What is your name? *

Your answer

Your email address *

Your answer

What is the name of your school or university?

Your answer

Which lessons do you want? *

- ☐ Access Matters
- ☐ Ask the Right Questions
- ☐ Citations
- ☐ Question Authority
- ☐ Scholarly Conversations
- ☐ Search Strategies
- ☐ Types of Information
- ☐ Value of Information

What kind of links do you want? *

LTI is for recording grades directly into your LMS (Canvas, Blackboard, D2L, etc.) Score Center is for

Assessment

The wider implementation, particularly in the first year, is still a testing phase. Integrating assessment into the release allows the committee to identify and address both concerns about and benefits of the program. Assessment also serves as a public relations tool to respond to stakeholders who do not welcome the learning objects. Whether they are frustrated by the technology, unhappy with the perceived burden of changing an established course's pedagogy, or unimpressed by a perceived lack of impact on student learning, you will have disgruntled stakeholders. An assessment program that not only solicits feedback but also addresses concerns can go a long way toward improving the reception of your learning objects. Your assessment plan should include public reports regarding the impact on student learning. An assessment program also provides further opportunities to partner with other faculty, as they may be interested in conducting and publishing research with you about using the learning objects. See chapter 7 for more information on an assessment program.

Implementation in Practice

The NLA's initial implementation plan involved a comprehensive suite of learning objects that would be managed through a centralized dashboard, allowing student scores to follow students from class to class or, if they transferred, institution to institution. We invested several years working toward this goal before reevaluating. While we had several learning objects and a dashboard prototype, we did not have the programming resources to fully realize the dashboard. During a meeting between the steering committee and our sponsors, we established a new plan: implement six learning objects within six months, using our existing software to distribute or embed learning objects in LMSs. This shift to rolling out a minimum viable product—that is, the baseline of what would meet our needs—reenergized the project. Between the completed learning objects and those in process, at the end of six months we had a suite of learning objects that covered the most common content taught by librarians in classes. We committed to rolling out learning objects twice a year. The dashboard is still part of our long-term plan but no longer holds up the implementation.

The new plan meant that our learning objects would be implemented à la carte, at least initially, so we did not have to obtain permissions beyond those from our own libraries and from teaching partners. We already had total support from our library administrators.

We conducted a soft launch at the course level using the six developed learning objects. Two librarians each from two institutions (four librarians total) tested the learning objects with at least one course or program each during the same spring semester. The librarians had established relationships with the course instructors and were familiar with the course content. The learning objects were integrated at different times in the semester, dependent upon the course.

We collected anecdotal and factual data to assess the soft launch. Librarians reported how they adjusted their classes in response to the learning objects. We conferred with course instructors about how the learning objects functioned as assignments and learned that we needed more than two or three assessment questions. We reviewed data recording how long students took to complete the learning objects to confirm the learning objects could be completed within our goal time of eight to fifteen minutes. In an ideal world, this would have been a formal assessment process with a report recording questions, results, and next steps. Given time and staff constraints, we were less structured and more iterative in our process. As issues arose, we addressed them and, if needed, modified our procedures.

Our wider implementation has focused on providing librarians across our institutions with the resources to market and integrate learning objects into classes. This includes creating a primer, moving our website to a new server with its own URL, and marketing learning objects to whole departments rather than individual faculty. We have also been asked to focus more on implementing the learning objects in other venues, such as research guides (see figure 5.4 for an example), so we are updating our documentation and resources. Some superstar librarians have already integrated the learning objects into degree programs. As an added implementation layer, our learning objects are freely available under a Creative Commons license. This created another set of workflows and data collection to be managed. We are also embarking on assessment, first focusing on a qualitative assessment involving our teaching faculty and students who have completed the learning objects.

FIGURE 5.4

Screenshot from Fort Hays State University LibGuide

So, how have the learning objects affected logistics and pedagogies for library instruction? Thus far, librarians are initiating their use. For example, a librarian was contacted about working with an undergraduate course in English during the fall semester. The librarian requested the syllabus and/or the associated research assignment. Based on these documents, the librarian recommended assigning two NLA learning objects: "Search Strategies" and "Types of Information." The learning objects were assigned as homework to be completed by the day the librarian met with the class. The learning objects were embedded in the course LMS and the librarian was granted access. Because we had to obtain links for the learning objects and make them available to students in order to complete them prior to the library class, we needed at least one week to incorporate learning objects into the class.

The librarian developed the library class to focus on strategically searching in literature-specific databases. The learning objects covered developing keywords, refining searches, and evaluating sources. The librarian designed hands-on activities so students could practice those skills. These activities included developing keywords for a research topic as a class and pairing students to search for relevant articles in different databases using the same research topic. Instead of demonstrating each database, the librarian assigned a database to each pair of students and challenged them to search. While the students searched, the librarian walked through the room, observing techniques and guiding students through challenges. Then, each pair reported to the class about their database, assessing how relevant the source was, describing how they refined their searches, and offering general search methods. Several groups offered search methods that the librarian would not have, just due to concerns about information overload.

With more experience using the NLA learning objects, librarians have identified pedagogical changes to their in-person classes, including these:

- Incorporating more hands-on time
- Creating more opportunities for students to share search and evaluation methods
- Integrating more discipline-specific research methods
- Increased focus on evaluating information

CRITICAL QUESTIONS

1. What types of approval or permissions are necessary in order to implement your project?

2. What models and institutional resources exist to help you navigate the approval process?

3. What information or resources can be shared between institutions to facilitate gaining approval?

4. Whom do you need to work with outside the project team in order to implement the learning objects?

5. What deadlines do you have to meet?

6. How long do you anticipate it will take to implement your project?

7. How will the data collected be managed?

8. What do you need to learn from a soft rollout?

9. How does your project help faculty/students do whatever they are doing, better?

10. Who are your audiences?

11. What information do they need to know?

12. What pedagogical guidance do your teaching partners need in order to use the learning objects?

13. What logistical information/resources do your partners need in order to use the learning objects?

14. How will you troubleshoot or provide technical support for the learning objects?

References

ACRL (Association of College & Research Libraries). 2016. *Framework for Information Literacy for Higher Education.* Chicago: American Library Association. www.ala.org/acrl/standards/ilframework.

Goddard, Robert. 1921. "That Moon Rocket Proposition: Its Proponent Says a Few Words in Refutation of Some Popular Fallacies." *Scientific American* 124 (9): 166.

Potter, Ned. 2012. *The Library Marketing Toolkit.* London: Facet.

US Department of Education. 2015. "Family Educational Rights and Privacy Act (FERPA)." Last modified June 26. www2.ed.gov/policy/gen/guid/fpco/ferpa/index.html.

Technical Parameters

6

In This Chapter

- ✓ Software Options
- ✓ Hosting and Usage
- ✓ Technical Constraints
- ✓ Platform and Software Analysis
- ✓ Technical Parameters in Practice

*The art challenges the technology, and
the technology inspires the art.*

—John Lasseter (2012)

CHECKLIST

- ☐ Determine where learning objects are to be hosted.
- ☐ Ensure ADA (Americans with Disabilities Act) accessibility.
- ☐ Complete feature/functionality list.
- ☐ Plan to analyze software.

Selecting the right technology for building learning objects is an important decision, but it is just one of many to thoughtfully consider when determining the technical parameters of your project. Technical considerations should occur in tandem with the online learning object planning phase of your project. It is important to determine how you want your learning objects to look and function first and then choose a software product or combination of products to meet those goals. You should also think about the technical aspects of implementation, hosting, and accessibility of your learning objects after the design process is complete. This chapter covers the basic technical considerations of collaborative learning object creation, starting with a look at software options, followed by hosting and usage considerations, and then a closer look at technical constraints and analyses.

Software Options

There are myriad tools to choose from when developing tutorials. Often a combination of these tools is used to produce the final product. You must

FIGURE 6.1

Software Considerations

Desired Effect/ Functionality	Type of Tool or Technology	Common Examples with Price Estimates	Learning Curve
Capturing movements on a screen or webcam	Video and screencasting	Screencast-O-Matic: free	Low
		Jing: free	Low
		Snagit: $	Medium
		Camtasia Studio: $$	High
		Adobe Captivate: $$$	High
Static images	Image/graphics editor	Paint.NET: free on PC	Low
		GIMP: free	Medium
		Snagit: $	Medium
		Photoshop: $$$	High
Moving images such as whiteboard-style or illustrations	Animation or live-action video	Blender: free	High
		PowToon: $	Medium
		VideoScribe: $$	Medium
		Adobe Animate CC: $$$	High

decide if you want videos, images, and/or interactivity in your learning objects. What you choose depends on your budget, skill set, and the goals for your final product. Some options to consider include those listed in figure 6.1.

Consider purchasing a design product that allows you to create packaged learning objects with a combination of features, such as videos, interactive elements, and assessments. Design software is expensive and has a steep learning curve but can produce high-quality learning experiences for your patrons and students. Design products also typically render learning objects in formats that can sync with LMSs or content management systems like LibGuides. SoftChalk Cloud, Smart Sparrow, Acrobatiq, and Elucidat are all examples of learning object design products currently on the market.

Hosting and Usage

Hosting is one of the first technical considerations to ponder in a collaborative curriculum environment. The major questions to ask at this stage are as follows:

- Who will need access to the learning objects and how will they use them?
- Are you going to collect assessment data and, if yes, where will you store it?
- Where will the learning objects need to live in order to facilitate access and assessment?

There are many options for hosting digital learning objects. They can, for example, be embedded into LibGuides, uploaded to YouTube, and synched with courses in LMSs, among many other options. The hosting question becomes trickier when you add in the element of assessment and how you collect and/or share the score data with your partners.

On the simple end, several learning object design products are LTI-compliant (discussed in more detail in the later Portability section): the responses to assessment questions can be synched with a grade book inside an LMS and exported if needed for further analysis. On the more complicated end, you may want to compile assessment data from various uses at multiple institutions, in which case it might be easier to host the learning objects and collect the data in the cloud, using software designed to collect assessment data, such as the SoftChalk ScoreCenter. In any case, if collecting assessment data, check with your campus FERPA experts to ensure that you are not violating privacy laws. Spend some time thinking about hosting and usage before you get too far into the project or you may run into more technical snags than you anticipated when you are ready to release your learning objects.

Accessibility

There is some truly beautiful and amazing learning design software with sophisticated interfaces and functionality. Not all such options are accessible for people with disabilities.

The Americans with Disabilities Act (ADA) and, if the government entities receive federal funding, the Rehabilitation Act of 1973 generally require that state and local governments provide qualified individuals with disabilities equal access to their programs, services, or activities unless doing so would fundamentally alter the nature of their programs, services, or activities or would impose an undue burden (US Department of Justice, 2016, § 35.149, § 35.164). This means that not only the content and visual elements included in learning objects must be accessible, but also any navigation, interactive elements, and assessment questions, including the hosting platform itself.

Larger campuses often have offices focused on accessibility and access issues for students with disabilities. Contact your office before starting a large design project. The federal government maintains information and technical assistance on the Americans with Disabilities Act at www.ada.gov. A complete "Software Accessibility Checklist," available from the US Department of Justice (2015), includes the following questions and many more:

- Does the product provide keyboard equivalents for all mouse actions, including buttons, scroll windows, text entry fields, and pop-up windows?
- Does every window, object, and control have a clearly named label?
- Can the user disable or adjust sound volume?
- Can the user adjust or disable flashing, rotating, or moving displays?

It can be tempting to choose the most visually appealing or functionally spectacular product in the early phases of design, but you should ensure that basic accessibility requirements are met in order to design learning content for all potential users.

For example, drag-and-drop activities can be fun and engaging but are not typically accessible for those using keyboard navigation or screen readers to access content. Early iterations of NLA learning objects utilized the drag-and-drop tool shown in figure 6.2 before we tried to tab through the activity.

> **TIP**
>
> Even drag-and-drop exercises designed to be keyboard accessible are difficult to use for those who utilize keyboard navigation or screen readers to access online content.

FIGURE 6.2

SoftChalk Drag-and-Drop Activity

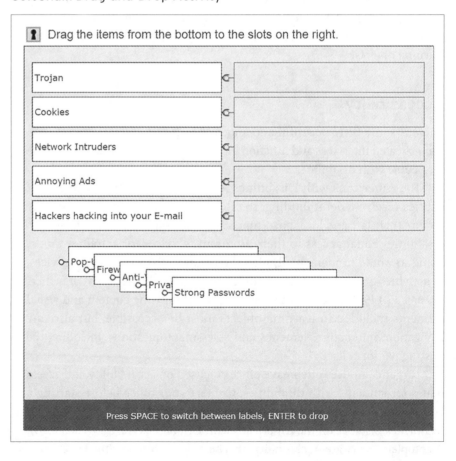

Portability

It is challenging to determine the scope and reach of an instructional design project meant to be shared, especially outside of your own institution. But this is one consideration that merits special attention because the software with which you build learning objects determines how portable the learning objects will be. That is, can the learning objects be used at multiple institutions even if they use different systems? When selecting learning object design software, consider whether the learning objects will interact with multiple software types and systems or just one. For example, there are many LMSs in place across colleges and universities, ranging from small, home-grown systems to large, full-featured products like Blackboard and Canvas. While not every system functions the same, there are tools that support portability. Three examples are API, SCORM, and LTI:

> **Application programming interface (API)** is a set of routines, protocols, and tools for building software that specifies how software components should interact. Tools like LibGuides, Google, and other platforms increasingly use APIs to help their systems interact seamlessly with other systems.

> **Sharable Content Object Reference Model (SCORM)** is a format that "integrates a set of related technical standards, specifications, and guidelines designed to meet SCORM's high-level requirements—accessible, interoperable, durable, and reusable content and systems" (Advanced Distributed Learning 2011).

> **Learning Tools Interoperability (LTI)** is a protocol similar to SCORM that is meant to establish a standard way of integrating rich learning applications with platforms like LMSs, portals, learning object repositories, or other educational environments (IMS Global 2017).

The NLA currently uses SoftChalk, which is LTI-compliant, meaning the assessments we create in each learning object can sync with a course gradebook within most LMSs. We have relied heavily on LTI compliance for synchronization with partner LMSs and will include LTI compliance as a required criteria in future platform analyses.

Technical Constraints

In an era of shrinking budgets and increased reliance on low-cost solutions to tough problems, it can be difficult to identify the right technology for your project. Before you decide, consider the short-term and long-term constraints you might face.

IT Support

Consider the investment of time and resources needed from your IT department. Consult with your IT managers before you choose a product to ensure that it will sync with existing technologies, server specifications, operating systems, and protocols. The code and specifications behind many lesson-building platforms are complicated, and you do not want any surprises when you finally get to the building and implementation stages of your project. It is also important to consider how much customization and installation time might be needed to get an out-of-the-box product to function in an ideal manner.

Technical Skills

Take an honest look at your technical skills or those of the individuals who will be working directly with the software. Will it take many hours of training or tutorials to learn how to use it effectively? Consider trialing several products at the same time. If you will be collecting assessment data, create questions in each program and see how they work. Try embedding the learning objects in an LMS or LibGuide. If you feel comfortable with multiple products, get a second opinion from someone who is less comfortable with them but who might use the products to build learning objects.

Functionality

Of course, you want the best product with the most features and the most attractive interface. But chances are you will not find all of your desired functionality and features in the same product, and if you do, it might not be affordable. Develop a list of the nonnegotiable product features and functionalities for your project to compare with the features list of the products you evaluate.

Licensing

How many people will be using the software? Check the licensing restrictions of products. Some companies require that extra licenses be purchased if the software will be used at multiple institutions or have user number caps on individual licenses. Ask your IT representatives for help in deciphering contract language if you are uncertain about the terms.

Platform and Software Analysis

Once you have a good idea about hosting, usage, and possible technical constraints, you are ready to conduct a software/platform analysis. Take your list of nonnegotiable features and functionalities and expand it into a specifications document that includes the most you can pay for the product up front and annually, how much time you can devote to setting up and learning the new software, an accessibility checklist, and where and how you intend to host the learning objects when they are completed. This section covers some additional factors to consider in your analysis.

Cost

Realistic cost analyses can help you get more life out of your technology and can help provide a stable environment for building and/or hosting learning objects.

- How much can you afford to spend on technology now and in the years to come?
- If you are funding the project with a grant, will the grant funds cover the cost of the product you want or will you need to compromise on important functionalities?
- If you subscribe to a product annually, can you reasonably expect your software budget to remain stable over the life of the project?

Longevity

Consider the life of the project. Short-term projects might require very different technical specifications than long-term ones. Consider also whether students or users might have repeated exposure to the learning objects or platform over time. It is important to weigh learning object consistency with the benefits of product migration. Also important to think about is the long-term stability of the product you are considering. Investigate how long the company has been in business, read external reviews of the product, and check out development forums that hint at how responsive their development team is in addressing technical issues.

- How long do you intend the project to last?
- Do you anticipate moving to a new technology if one with better features or functionalities comes along?
- How long might project partners continue their participation?

Usability

What you might find beautiful, functional, or helpful might not be received as such by your potential target audience. While you are trialing potential products, conduct a small usability test with a few members of your project's target audience on each product using some filler content. Ask your students what they like about it, what they hate about, and their preferences among products. Such data may be helpful in making a final determination if you find that multiple products meet your baseline specifications.

FIGURE 6.3

Platform Analysis Template

Executive Summary
Overview of Required Criteria
Overview of Platforms Selected for Analysis
Evaluation of Each Platform

	Platform 1	Platform 2	Platform 3
Company Information			
Summary of Product			
Required Criteria Scores/ Evaluation			
Strengths/Weaknesses			
Summary			

Final Recommendation

Use the template shown in figure 6.3 or one of your own design to compile your platform analysis.

The analysis should be easy to read and effectively demonstrate the need for your chosen platform or technology, especially if you will have to justify the cost of the platform to administrators or IT representatives. A side-by-side comparison of each platform is helpful to capture the analysis, especially for those who might be inclined to skip the details and get straight to the point. Figure 6.4 presents an excerpt from the first NLA platform analysis conducted in 2012.

FIGURE 6.4

NLA Platform Analysis Excerpt

Platform	URL	Comments
SoftChalk Cloud	https://softchalkcloud.com	Not a true LMS but an authoring tool that is combined with a cloud storage and management system. This allows each institution to keep its LMS and simply implement the learning objects as it sees fit. Supports options for the synching of grades and assessments. Is used already by several institutions in the consortium, with or without the cloud storage option.
Dokeos	www.dokeos.com/en	An activity-based LMS designed with usability in mind. Has support for tablets and other mobile devices and is coded in HTML5. Issues regarding requirement for centralized hosting at an institution that is shared across all consortium members. Does have its own quiz and lesson builder that has many activities and modules similar to SoftChalk. Steep learning curve and would require additional resources to maintain.
Lectora Online	www.trivantis.com/online-e-learning	Competitor to SoftChalk Cloud, not as popular as SoftChalk and is costlier than other authoring software. Does have a cloud-based system with management capabilities, yet would require more of an investment from consortium members in terms of resources and cost. Is considered secondary in market value when compared to SoftChalk.
Moodle	https://moodle.org	Open-source LMS that is popular in the higher education field. Has a great community and reputable stability, with several institutions globally using the product. Is not as full-featured as many paid LMS products and still brings up the issue of authoring content.
Chamilo	www.chamilo.org	Open-source LMS based off of the same code as Dokeos yet on a different project path. Chamilo focuses more on educational institutions, while Dokeos focuses on training and businesses. Has similar strengths and weaknesses to Dokeos but is more stable and has more options for customization.
Open edX	http://code.edx.org	Open-source course publishing software developed by Stanford, Google, UC Berkeley, Harvard, MIT, and the University of Queensland. Programmed in Python and available for customization and local adaptation through the AGPL (Affero General Public License). Includes Reporting and Analytics features. Supports local hosting only.
Google Classroom	www.google.com/edu/classroom	A simplified LMS similar to Moodle, Blackboard, or Canvas. Works only in connection with Google Apps for Education. Local hosting or hosting with Google is possible. Designed for the creation and distribution of online classroom assignments, not for the building of online lessons. Does not support LTI or SCORM.
Smart Sparrow	www.smartsparrow.com	A relatively new addition to the market of online learning platforms and a major competitor to other platforms, such as SoftChalk Cloud. A cloud-based system with an easy-to-use content creation shell. While lesson creation is flash-based, all lessons can be rendered in HTML5. Works on mobile devices. Pricing is higher than other comparable systems.

Include IT representatives in the analysis process so they are invested in your project at a higher level and can advise you on how the systems you are considering will integrate with existing systems on your or partner campuses.

Technical Parameters in Practice

The NLA has performed two platform analyses in the past five years: an initial analysis to determine the right tool for our work and a subsequent market analysis to ensure the product we are using is the best fit. The following criteria were used to measure each prospective platform.

SCORM compliance   It is recommended that the final collaborative product be SCORM-compliant to allow any lessons, courses, modules, activities, or other related instructional materials to be "plug and play" in terms of implementation across a broad spectrum of LMSs.

Assessments and statistics   The ideal platform needs to allow the tracking of grades, assessments, and other related statistics that are required to draw meaningful conclusions about the status of the product. Furthermore, analysis of these statistics and assessments will support the constant process of revision and adaptation that occurs with any lesson plan. At minimum, the platform needs to track grades and some form of statistics that can be shared with the collaborative and to permit collaborative members to keep track of grades from within their own LMSs.

Reporting   In this measurement index, it is paramount that the desired platform allows the population of statistics and grading reports in a manner that can easily be migrated to a usable format. Such reports can be shared in a manner that provides no additional workload to any institution and provides for seamless integration with institution-based assessments.

Customized learning content   Learning content will follow standards based on the desired outcomes and objectives of the collaborative's focus; however, such learning content must be customizable to ensure it matches the needs of each individual institution involved.

Expandability   A platform that is unable to be upgraded, adapted, or expanded to meet the ever-changing needs of students and respond efficiently to changes in technology is undesirable. For this reason, each platform chosen has an active development community (or company responsible for development) and can be expanded (adapted) in some fashion.

During both analyses, we determined that SoftChalk Cloud was the right tool for our purposes. The NLA supports a combination of hosting options for potential partner institutions. We work with institutions and faculty who want their students to complete our learning objects in the cloud through SoftChalk, our platform for both building and hosting learning objects, and also with those who prefer to embed the learning objects into their courses and LibGuides.

We also use SoftChalk's ScoreCenter to collect score data for learning objects that we use for internal assessment, which is further described in chapter 7. We have found SoftChalk to be relatively versatile with regard to synchronization in these environments. Figure 6.5 shows a learning object on the SoftChalk platform.

This cloud-based product requires only a small degree of technical knowledge to use it out of the box, so we do not have to rely on our IT departments for anything but the licensing agreements. We have spent considerable time testing and creating instructions for use of the learning objects within LMS courses because LTI synchronization typically requires several steps.

FIGURE 6.5

NLA Learning Object Embedded in a LibGuide

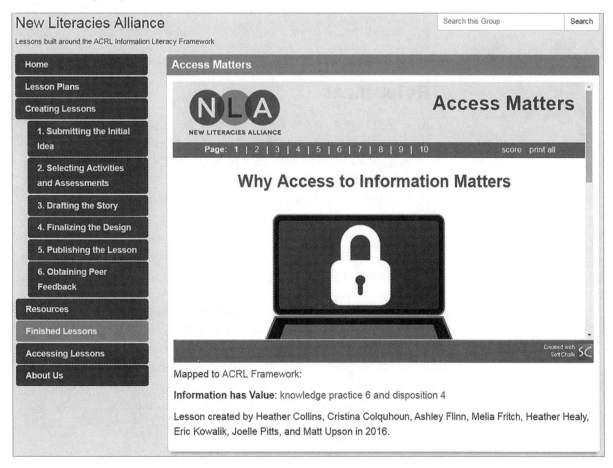

Each license costs several hundred dollars per year, depending on use, and the product has been stable over time, allowing us to consistently afford the subscription and to learn how to customize our content. Although we find the interface and navigation do not meet all of our expectations, the LTI compliance and back-end assessment data collection capabilities have made this our technology of choice for the time being.

CRITICAL QUESTIONS

1. Who will need access to the learning objects and how will they use them?

2. Are you going to collect assessment data and, if yes, where will you store it?

3. Where will the learning objects need to live in order to facilitate access and assessment?

4. Does the product you are considering meet ADA and Section 508 requirements?

5. What technical constraints are you working under, such as available IT support and technical skills of your project staff?

6. What are the minimum features and functionalities you need in a software package to achieve your project goals?

7. How much can you afford to spend up front and annually on software and hosting?

References

Advanced Distributed Learning. 2011. *SCORM User's Guide for Instructional Designers.* 4th ed., version 8. ADLnet.gov, January 15. adlnet.gov/wp-content/uploads/2011/12/SCORM_Users_Guide_for _ISDs.pdf.

IMS Global. 2017. "Learning Tools Interoperability Background." Accessed March 29. www.imsglobal.org/activity/learning-tools -interoperability.

Lasseter, John. 2012. "John Lasseter on the Future of Animation." Speech delivered at the Academy's Development of the Digital Animator, Samuel Goldwyn Theater, Beverly Hills, CA, May 21. Accessed March 31, 2017. https://youtu.be/uFbOOjAC_Fg.

US Department of Justice. 2015. "Software Accessibility Checklist." Updated August 6. www.justice.gov/crt/software-accessibility-checklist.

———. 2016. "Americans with Disabilities Act Title II Regulations." As amended by the final rule published August 11. www.ada.gov/ regs2010/titleII_2010/titleII_2010_regulations.htm.

Assessment

7

In This Chapter

✓ Assessing Student Learning
✓ Assessing Online Learning Modules
✓ Assessment in Practice

TERMS

Formative assessment   Evaluation and feedback used to help the learner improve (Kern, Thomas, and Hughes 2009).

Open educational resources (OERs)   Teaching resources of any medium or size that are freely shared (Creative Commons 2016); can refer to multiple items combined together, such as a learning object, or to a single individual component (graphic, video, poll, quiz, activity, etc.).

Summative assessment   Evaluation used to verify achievement, make judgments, or assign a grade (Kern, Thomas, and Hughes 2009).

CHECKLIST

☐ Identify student learning tools.

☐ Identify project assessment tools.

☐ Plan for implementing assessments.

☐ Set scoring options and technologies.

☐ Establish a process for sharing/ providing scores.

☐ Plan for closing the loop and demonstrating value.

> *What kind of experts do you think your school*
> *is creating and how would you know?*
>
> —Nicole Woods (2016)

You will need to collect consistent data from multiple areas to inform strategic directions and demonstrate the value of your project to stakeholders. As a part of academia, you are beholden not only to accrediting bodies but also to governmental leaders, taxpayers, alumni, workforce arenas, professional organizations, and, of course, students and their families (Praslova 2010). Your assessment plans for online instructional projects must demonstrate value and accountability not only to students but also to stakeholders (Oakleaf 2010). Your project's value is ultimately measured by student learning metrics. Optimally, your students' content knowledge and skill mastery will become a foundation for observable behavior (Praslova 2010). In addition to assessing learning outcomes, you can also consider assessing other areas, such as program efficiency, cost savings, or cultural impact.

In setting out to assess student learning and your project, identify the data needed and how that data will inform your next steps. Assessment data needs to be actionable. Your assessment practices should be rigorous, but bear in mind that this is not pure research. The assessment strategies discussed here are meant to provide milestones for programs and learning. They inform student learning progress, provide insight into ways that you can improve your project, and assist in demonstrating impact to stakeholders. Assessment is an ongoing process with many moving parts, one which will benefit from your planning and management skills.

Assessment should be incorporated into all stages of the project and tied closely to the design process. When you start out, decide which student learning metrics will be collected and which data will show programmatic impact. In order to procure and maintain resources to support your work, your data must demonstrate meaningful contributions to your university's strategic vision. Countless scholarly works address library and academic assessment, but here we provide practical strategies for assessing and reporting on student learning in an online environment.

Assessing Student Learning

No one tool or strategy fully assesses student learning. You will need to use several assessment approaches together to tell a broader story and look at learning from multiple angles. The biggest pitfall in selecting assessment measures is focusing on educational *inputs* instead of learning *outputs*. For example, counting the minutes students spend in class (input measure) does not assess how well the students grasped the material. Output measures, such as a formative or summative assessment activity, are much more useful.

Within the *Framework for Information Literacy in Higher Education*, each of the six frames includes knowledge practices, "proficiencies or abilities that learners develop as a result of their comprehending a threshold concept," and dispositions, the "tendency to act or think in a particular way . . . preferences, attitudes and intentions" (ACRL 2016). Both knowledge practices and dispositions can be used as the foundation of outcomes-based assessments of student learning. Dispositions are by far more difficult to assess than knowledge practices, especially within short learning objects. However, to a large extent, it is possible, and behaviors ultimately demonstrate a higher level of learning.

À la Carte Assessment

Learning objects can be easily reorganized to assess student learning in different ways. Keep in mind that one of the primary characteristics of learning objects is their flexibility. The activities inside a learning object (videos, graphics, polls, quizzes, etc.) can be arranged and rearranged, added or deleted like beads on a string. You have the power to fully customize the assessment experience for the learner.

You also have many choices for implementing learning objects in different ways, and each way can lead to different assessment strategies. For

FIGURE 7.1

Learning Object Assessment Options

Instructional Timing	Grading Approach	Purpose
Learning object prior to class	Not graded	Formative instruction Introduction of content Supplemental resource
	Graded	Guided instruction in preparation of active learning or discipline-specific application
Classroom activity prior to learning object	Not graded	Student reflection Review
	Graded	Summative assessment
Learning object prior to other online activities	Not graded	Supplemental resource Online badge collection Specialized certificate of achievement
	Graded	Integrated element of online coursework

TIP Do not re-create the wheel! Before creating content, look for OERs related to the *Framework*, library instruction, and/or other subject areas to insert into your projects.

example, by asking students to complete a pass-fail *Framework*-based learning object before an in-person class, you will know if students have grasped the threshold concepts (ACRL 2016) before delving into discipline-specific applications in class. This approach also reserves in-class time for active learning. The chart in figure 7.1 demonstrates possible timings, grading options, and uses of learning objects. Keep in mind that the scoring of a learning object can be easily turned on or off, offered as pass-fail, or simply recorded "complete." This chart describes some of the more common assessment strategies for learning objects.

Scoring Technologies

As discussed in chapter 6, some learning object design software programs can record assessment data for individual activities or comprehensively. Elements such as digital badging, differentiated learning paths, and gating to differentiated content can be incorporated into assessment strategies.

While the possibilities for configuring digital scoring are endless, there are some common barriers you will likely run into. Student privacy rights require that formal agreements and approvals are obtained in order to share and store student data (US Department of Education 2015). Additionally, technologies that track students' progress across multiple courses, programs, and institutions (e.g., LRNG, www.lrng.com; Acrobatiq, www.acrobatiq.com; Knewton Adaptive Learning, www.knewton.com/approach; Smart Sparrow, www.smartsparrow.com) are less common and often prohibitively expensive. Nonetheless, they are needed now more than ever. Current national statistics show that almost 37.2 percent of college students who entered school in 2008 transferred institutions at least once, with almost half of that population having transferred multiple times. This accounted for approximately 2.4 million transfers between 2008 and 2014 (National Student Clearinghouse Research Center 2015).

Although transfers are increasing, one of the biggest challenges and opportunities for instruction librarians lies in the fact that most professional (discipline-based) accrediting bodies do not require the *Framework*. As a consequence, there is no pressure to teach or track students' mastery of the *Framework* interinstitutionally. If you have formed a consortium with members from institutions that students frequently transfer between, one option would be to work out the technical and administrative logistics to create a scoring system that would track students' progress in light of the *Framework*.

NLA's Scoring Technologies

The NLA created a prototype of a dashboard that would enable individual students to create accounts and assessment data that would follow a student across multiple instructors, across programs, and even between institutions. While not yet fully realized, this solution would enable institutions to formally track metaliteracy competencies while anticipating the challenges of an increasingly more transient student population.

Currently, the NLA shares online lessons through Creative Commons Attribution-NonCommercial-ShareAlike licenses. Lessons reside in the

FIGURE 7.2

LTI Data Transfer Diagram

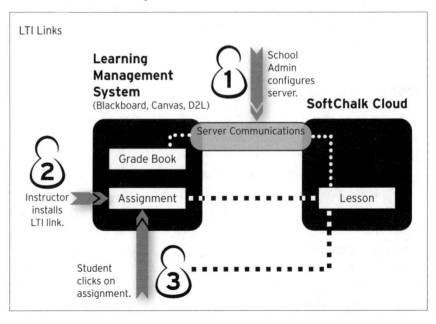

SoftChalk Cloud for librarians and instructors to (1) download, (2) integrate into LMSs, or (3) obtain hyperlinks to the lessons (NLA 2017). NLA instructional designers assist librarians in obtaining scored or unscored NLA content. Assistance can be requested through the NLA website, www .newliteraciesalliance.org. Figure 7.2 demonstrates options for obtaining and using NLA's online lessons.

Assessing Online Learning Modules

Review lessons multiple times and with various tools and processes. Depending on the scope of your project, you may decide to use all of the following assessments, add others, or select the few that best inform your work.

Team-Based Creation

If you form teams to create learning objects, the process of collaborating and the support of peers act as a type of peer review. Forming diverse teams with members who have multiple areas of expertise enhances the review of the learning object.

Rapid Prototyping

As part of the rapid prototyping process described in chapter 4, each learning object you create should be tested with members of the target audience. These tests should be uniform across your project (i.e., all testers should be asked the same questions, they should be tested in the same format and under the same conditions, and all tests should be recorded for each learning object).

In practice: When the NLA conducts rapid prototyping, the students' digital experience is recorded for later viewing. This experience and their written feedback is color-coded into spreadsheets. Instructional designers then collate this data into a report for the content creators and other team members (see appendix G for an excerpt of this report). This report helps the team finalize the learning object. Later, we analyze all the reports from all the various teams together to observe trends and other issues that may affect future design timelines and processes. We review these reports periodically to reflect on the learning objects being created as well as the health of the project. Each report consists of the following:

- Demographic information
- Reported confidence with the lesson content
- Time each tester took to finish the lesson and average time for all testers
- Answers to each assessment question

- Truncated verbal responses to each question
- Action items based on the feedback (see appendix H for the rapid prototyping student response form)

Usability Testing Checklist

Use the checklist provided here to improve the usability of your learning objects, but keep in mind that additional criteria will likely be needed as you work through your content.

USABILITY TESTING CHECKLIST

Navigation

- ☐ Links are easily accessible and clear in their purpose and destination.
- ☐ Content conforms to Internet and ADA standards.
- ☐ There are no broken links and no inaccessible navigation.
- ☐ Most important links or tasks are highlighted and emphasized for the user.
- ☐ Links are obvious and take the user to relevant content.
- ☐ Links will explicitly inform the user if they are external, require a certain software program, or link to a file.
- ☐ There are no generic descriptions, such as "Click Here," before a link.
- ☐ It is clear to users where they are within the learning object.
- ☐ The table of contents page is easily located.
- ☐ Load time is minimal for each page within the learning object.

User Interaction

- ☐ Tasks require the minimum amount of input possible from the user.
- ☐ Users understand where to go and what to do on each page of the learning object.
- ☐ Users are able to navigate and interact with the learning object by relying on recognition, not recall or memorization.
- ☐ Actions performed within the learning object make sense to the user.
- ☐ Interface functions provide meaningful context to the user and are not confusing.
- ☐ All learning outcomes and objectives are met by task-oriented assessment that demonstrates learner success in these areas.

Text

- ☐ Language is nontechnical and appropriate for the audience.
- ☐ Title tags, heading text, and URLs are clear and descriptive.
- ☐ Text is clear, easy to read/scan, and free of errors.
- ☐ Abbreviations, acronyms, and so forth, are spelled out and defined.
- ☐ Consistent capitalization and grammar are used.
- ☐ Command sentences are used only for mandatory tasks; qualifying statements are used elsewhere.

Layout

- ☐ Essential content on a page is viewable on various screen sizes.
- ☐ Design, layout, and organization of the learning object are consistent, professional, and aesthetically pleasing.
- ☐ Drop-down menus are not used unless necessary.

Style

- ☐ Heavy contrast is used between text and background colors.
- ☐ Color choices for the learning object allow for easy readability.

Content

- ☐ Redundant content is avoided.
- ☐ Animation is never used alone to cover critical concepts.
- ☐ The content is up-to-date, authoritative, and trustworthy.
- ☐ Labels and tags for graphics and images are meaningful.
- ☐ Content appears the same across all browsers.
- ☐ Images, videos, audio, files, and other technologies enrich the message and do not present access barriers.

Learning Object Rubric

Create a peer-review process and use a rubric like the one in appendix E to evaluate the final learning object.

Reviewing Scoring and Assessment Questions

After a pilot test of the learning object and periodically afterward, review the reliability and validity of the scored activities and assessment questions. The NLA reviewed the following scoring data, as shown in figure 7.3:

- Number of correct responses out of total responses
- Percentage of correct responses
- Most common wrong answer among all wrong answers

This analysis helped the assessment team create several recommendations for edits to questions with correct response rates below 90 percent. The group acknowledged that a small percentage of incorrect responses was normal and expected. The team chose 90 percent as the cut-off point because most responses fell in this range, but the outlying scores for your learning object may be different. Outlying questions were reviewed for clarity in wording, structure, and technological format as well as relevance to the content.

FIGURE 7.3

NLA Assessment Research

Lesson	Assessment Number	Correct Answers/ Total Answers	% Correct	Most Common Wrong Answer	% Occurrence of Most Common Wrong Answer
Right Questions	1	256/287	90	A	61
	2	260/292	89	ABC	38
	3	251/290	87	D	54
Search Strategies	1	254/271	94	D	35
	2	233/270	86	B	41
	3	249/270	92	D	24
Types of Information	1	270/280	96	B	65
	2	263/283	93	C	65

Faculty Feedback

Ideally, you will include faculty collaborators on your project. The ultimate impact and usefulness of your project will depend on its alignment with content and curricular needs. Periodically, conduct focus groups with faculty members and administrators, especially when in the process of strategic planning. Liberating Structures (www.liberatingstructures.com) provides many tools for conducting focus groups that will elicit constructive feedback.

Curriculum Mapping

A qualitative way to review the relevance of your project is to map discipline-specific competencies to the *Framework*. This enables you to identify gaps in the learning objects or in the curriculum that can be corrected with revisions or new learning objects. (See figure 3.1 in chapter 3 for an example of a curriculum map.)

Assessment in Practice

NLA members employed all of the aforementioned assessment strategies and continue to inform work through ongoing assessment practices. Two IRB reviews were obtained in order to conduct rapid prototyping and usability testing. Results of NLA's assessment work have been communicated at various scholarly conferences and in a variety of publications, but efforts are also frequently shared with NLA members and stakeholders as future plans evolve.

CRITICAL QUESTIONS

1. Do faculty report that the learning objects augment their course content?
2. How do learning object outcomes tie into existing standards and competencies?
3. Are the learning objects you build really teaching students to master outcomes you set?
4. How will the learning object be scored? (Will it be formatively or summatively assessed?)
5. How can student progress be tracked from one learning outcome to another, one course to another, and even one institution to another?
6. How will you assess the learning objects and what data will guide you in improving them?
7. How can a peer-review model improve project deliverables?
8. How can librarians demonstrate that learning objects improve departmental, programmatic, or university outcomes?

References

ACRL (Association of College & Research Libraries). 2016. *Framework for Information Literacy for Higher Education.* www.ala.org/acrl/standards/ilframework.

Creative Commons. 2016. "What Is OER?" Last modified February 8. https://wiki.creativecommons.org/wiki/What_is_OER%3F.

Kern, David E., Patricia A. Thomas, and Mark T. Hughes, eds. 2009. *Curriculum Development for Medical Education: A Six-Step Approach.* 2nd ed. Baltimore, MD: Johns Hopkins University Press.

Mackey, Thomas P., and Trudi E. Jacobson. 2011. "Reframing Information Literacy as a Metaliteracy." *College & Research Libraries* 72 (1): 62–78.

National Student Clearinghouse Research Center. 2015. *Transfer and Mobility: A National View of Student Movement in Postsecondary Institutions, Fall 2008 Cohort.* Signature Report 9. http://nscresearchcenter.org/signaturereport9.

NLA (New Literacies Alliance). 2017. "Get Lesson Links." Accessed March 31. http://newliteraciesalliance.org/using-lessons/get-lesson-links.

Oakleaf, Megan. 2010. *The Value of Academic Libraries: A Comprehensive Research Review and Report.* Chicago: Association of College and Research Libraries, American Library Association.

Praslova, Ludmila. 2010. "Adaptation of Kirkpatrick's Four Level Model of Training Criteria to Assessment of Learning Outcomes and Program Evaluation in Higher Education." *Educational Assessment, Evaluation and Accountability* 22 (3): 215–25.

US Department of Education. 2015. "Family Educational Rights and Privacy Act (FERPA)." Last modified June 26. www2.ed.gov/policy/gen/guid/fpco/ferpa/index.html.

Woods, Nicole. 2016. *Active Learning and Integration: Using Learning to Enhance Teaching.* Presentation on August 26 at the School of Medicine Faculty Retreat, The University of Kansas Medical Center, Kansas City, KS.

Long-Term Planning

8

TERMS

Stakeholder   One who is involved in or affected by a course of action (Merriam-Webster 2017).

Succession planning   Identification and development of potential successors for key positions in an organization, through a systematic evaluation process and training (BusinessDictionary 2017).

In This Chapter

✓ Content Maintenance

✓ Technology Review

✓ Funding

✓ Administrative and Stakeholder Support

✓ Project Leadership and Succession Planning

✓ Project Capacity

✓ Long-Term Planning in Practice

A goal without a plan is just a wish.
—Commonly attributed to
Antoine de Saint-Exupéry

Collaborative projects often hinge on two or three individuals or grants to get started and build momentum. However, grant-funded projects can fall apart after the funding runs out. Leaders within the group can move on or up. Administrations can shift, leaving projects in limbo or with a lower priority. Maintenance of the project as a whole is important to ensure the long-term viability of the learning objects. If you want all of your hard work and effort to live on in perpetuity, plan for it and structure your collaboration in a way that facilitates the long-term success and survival of your project. Identify your short- and long-term goals for the project and allocate project members and resources accordingly. This chapter presents some foundations of long-term collaborations.

CHECKLIST

☐ Establish a content and technology review schedule.

☐ Create a funding plan with your leadership team.

☐ Map your project's existing standards, outcomes, programs, and initiatives.

☐ Establish a succession plan.

Content Maintenance

Creating learning objects can take a huge commitment of time and resources, especially in a collaborative setting. After working for weeks, months, or even years on specific content, you may find it difficult to return to that content periodically to review and update it. It is imperative, however, that you plan for regular reviews of collaboratively created content to ensure the following:

- The content is up-to-date and still relevant to your audience.
- Links, navigation, and other elements are functioning properly and are still relevant.
- The assessments are still working to help your audience master the learning outcomes you have identified.
- Project collaborators or instructors are still using the content.

These reviews can occur on a timeline that works with the size and time commitments of your group and can include the original content creators or a brand-new group for individual learning objects. Another option is to establish a dedicated review committee to review all content at designated intervals. Regardless of how you structure the reviews, make sure the group agrees on the structure and that the process is embedded into the normal workflow of the project.

FIGURE 8.1

Learning Object Maintenance Checklist

Learning Object Name:

Created On:

Perform maintenance check twice per year.

	FA17	SP18	FA18	SP19	FA19
Accessibility					
Videos are captioned/transcribed.					
All components are keyboard accessible.					
All images have alternate text.					
Links					
All links are functional and lead to desired pages.					
All links open in new tabs.					
Content References					
References to current events are current within one year.					
References to digital interfaces and processes are current.					
Embedded Content (videos, polls, etc.)					
All embedded content functions as expected.					
Video screenshots highlight current interfaces.					
Learning Object Usage					
Record usage of the learning object by class and institution.					

Figure 8.1 is an example checklist that you can use to perform maintenance on your learning objects.

Technology Review

The technology you use to build and host your learning objects should also be periodically reviewed. Determine how often you will conduct a review. An arbitrary timeline such as every three or five years can work, but keep in mind that technology develops rapidly and new products enter the market every year. Features or functionalities that you compromised on early in the project may become commonly available or less expensive.

At every review interval, analyze your list of project goals and necessary functionalities that you created in chapter 6 to determine if those specifications still apply. Conduct a new software analysis, taking into account upgrades and new features of products you analyzed in prior reviews. It is helpful to have a broader understanding of educational technology trends in general as you embark on each review so that you can recognize which products are on the cutting edge. The annual *NMC Horizon Report* (www .nmc.org/nmc-horizon) is one way to glimpse the short-, mid-, and long-term trends in educational technology.

Funding

Funding for libraries and library projects can be a prickly issue, and you can expect many questions pertaining to sustainable funding to arise over the life of your collaborative project. Many libraries have struggled to balance the need for human resources and technology funding with the mission of providing learning objects and educational experiences for free to their communities. This balance is not easy to strike, and it often depends on a variety of factors related to both internal and external funding for the project.

Internal Funding: Partner Capacity and Resources

Consider what each project partner brings to the table in terms of technology, resources, available staff time, and skill sets. It is likely that some institutions will be able to support the project in larger measure than others. In some academic collaboratives, such as the Great Plains IDEA (2008) distance education consortium, a lead institution is identified and provides leadership and a financial home for grant funding. It is possible to rotate responsibility and resources among partner institutions, but more formalized agreements and documentation might be required for that type of model.

External Funding: Grants

Shrinking state and federal budget allocations to universities and libraries can make sustainable funding for collaborative projects difficult to achieve. Libraries are increasingly looking to granting agencies or other external funding sources to shore up the gaps. There are many granting agencies in existence, but it can be tough to find funding specifically for library instruction projects. The John S. and James L. Knight Foundation (www.knight foundation.org; News Challenge grants) and the Institute of Museum and Library Services (www.imls.gov) are examples of agencies that support library instruction projects. Grants databases such as COS (Community of Science) Pivot (http://pivot.cos.com/home/index) or Grant Forward (www .grantforward.com/index) can reveal other granting agencies. If you are lucky enough to have procured a grant to kick off your collaborative effort, consider early on how your institutional partners might help fund the project after grant funding dries up. Create a grant deadline calendar (see figure 8.2 for an example) that clearly outlines due dates and partner contributions to avoid last-minute scrambling.

The NLA steering committee applied for grant funding from the Knight Foundation and will pursue funding from other agencies. As the majority of the steering committee members were not experienced grant writers, the process was challenging, but it also was rewarding in that the project made it to the semifinal round of the 2016 Knight Foundation News Challenge grant-funding cycle. Using a grant calendar like the one shown in figure 8.2 helps keep deadlines and requirements organized for all grant-writing partners.

FIGURE 8.2

Grant Deadline Calendar

Grant Name	Proposal URL	Partner Assignments	Start Date	Submission Date	Decision Date
Knight Foundation News Challenge	www . . .	Member X: Member Y: Member Z:	2/1/2018	2/15/2018	March 2018
Institute of Museum and Library Services	www . . .	Member X: Member Y: Member Z:	3/15/2018	4/15/2018	May 2018
National Endowment for the Humanities	www . . .	Member X: Member Y: Member Z:	6/5/2018	7/1/2018	August 2018

Administrative and Stakeholder Support

Administrative Buy-In

You need library administrator buy-in and support from each institutional partner for your project to be successful:

- Philosophical support for the vision and goals of the project
- Human resource support in the form of encumbered staff lines and time
- Monetary support for software and marketing

It is important to communicate and get buy-in for the project from your upper administration early and often. Library deans, directors, and stakeholders at each partner institution/department/branch need to know about the project and the associated successes and barriers. Project reporting and impact narratives are especially important in communicating the value of the project during strategic planning, budgeting, and annual supervisory and workflow discussions. The same administrators also need to advise on the logistics and release of such a project at scale, and they will help hold the project team and their counterparts at partner institutions accountable for project success.

Early in the NLA project, the top administrators from both founding institutions helped to shape the foundation of the project and set goals for the steering committee. They continue to meet with the steering committee regularly to answer questions and provide guidance, especially with regard to long-term planning and resource allocation.

Stakeholder Support

Projects that align with institutional goals and strategic endeavors are more likely to receive attention and funding from administrators both within and outside of the library. Try to map your learning outcomes to those in your college's or university's core curriculum. Use the ACRL (2016) *Framework for Information Literacy for Higher Education* to create talking points with external departments that might turn into cross-departmental partnerships and funding sources. Contact your assessment office to determine how your project could align with organization-wide assessment and accreditation efforts. Even if these departments do not throw any money your way initially, those kinds of partnerships and awareness can lead to inclusion on large grants, increased collaboration with those who can speak for you in budget meetings, and perhaps increased priority placed on the project itself within the library. Throughout all of these efforts, document your conversations, the impact of each partnership over time, and the number of student and patron exposures to your project. Analyze and use this data to increase the reach and impact of your project.

Project Relevancy

Important for both library administration and project stakeholders is the need to regularly evaluate the relevancy of your project. Your team should consider the following two questions routinely:

- Does your project still align with current standards, objectives, and strategic plans?
- Is the content still relevant to the kinds of projects students are assigned in classes?

These questions are important to consider when reaching out to and communicating with administrators and stakeholders. Consider what action to take if the answer to either of those questions is "no."

Project Leadership and Succession Planning

Although two or three individuals or a grant can kick-start a design project and provide the momentum and energy required to carry a collaborative project for a few years, a stable and rotating leadership team is essential for long-term project viability. The steering committee should consist of individuals whose professional time has been encumbered into the project for a given time period or term. They should be excited about the project and willing to invest time and energy into helping the project continue and making it better overall. The project leadership structure should be organized and marketed as an opportunity for professional service. There were four founding members of the NLA project, two from K-State and two from KUMC. All four wrote the project into their annual performance plans and were supported by their administration to spend significant time on its creation. Subsequent members also worked with their supervisors to write the project into their monthly activities.

Rotation of the project leadership can help to extend the life of the project, bring new ideas, and infuse new energy into the project over time. There are many methods for project management and succession planning; determine the process that works best for your group. Consider the following questions:

- Where do you want the project to be in five years (vision)?
- What are your short-term and long-term objectives to achieve the vision?
- What skills and abilities will you need in your steering committee to achieve the vision?
- Who among your current members might be willing and able to serve on the steering committee?
- How often should the steering committee membership rotate and what is the process for determining new members?

There should also be a process in place to help new steering committee members learn the ropes and how they can best help the project move forward. Everyone should have access to and understand the marketing package and be able to represent the project to potential new members or teaching faculty. It is also helpful to review the elevator speech for the project together and make any updates or revisions.

Project Capacity

One of the major duties of the steering committee is to determine the capacity of the project for new content, new members, and new consumers of your content. These limits are often easier to recognize within a single library or institution but are trickier to establish in a collaborative environment. The steering committee must regularly evaluate the number and engagement level of project partners against the need for new content or other projects, such as regular content review, marketing, or assessment. When new partners join the effort, consider your existing capacity and defined projects that require participants. It is helpful not only to the steering committee but also to prospective members to be able to clearly articulate the scope and terms of project and small-group participation. The NLA website now hosts a "job board" page to describe the various project roles currently needing to be filled and how much time a prospective participant might anticipate spending on the project.

There is likely a limit to the number of partner institutions your project can feasibly handle with your current leadership and funding models. You should have a good feel for this limit, and also what your limits might be if you procure additional funding or personnel, such as project managers, software developers, instructional designers, or graphic design/marketing experts. You may also reach a point where you determine project membership based on building capacity in a particular area, such as instructional design or software development. When your steering committee grapples with the question of where you want the project to be in five years, strategically consider the capacity limitations you will likely face.

Long-Term Planning in Practice

The NLA has, at the time of this writing, ten lessons based on the *Framework* (at least one lesson mapped to each frame) and five lessons based on digital literacy concepts. The *Framework*-based lessons were made within the past two years and have not undergone a systematic review, yet. Three of the lessons were examined for student learning assessment and are currently being updated. And a recent accessibility check revealed that several lessons contained activities that were not keyboard accessible, so these were modified. A review of the older digital literacy lessons revealed that some updates were needed. Those lessons are currently unpublished and are on deck to be revised soon. We are beginning to track lesson use in more detail by using a combination of Google Analytics to record individual lesson statistics and communication with partner librarians and instructors to record data such as institution, faculty member, and class name, along with the number of students who take each lesson.

We are still working toward a sustainable funding model. The two founding institutions have made large investments in the form of staff time and technology, which are ongoing expenses. We are beginning to share some of the staff costs by inviting new partner institutions to help lead small-group efforts and projects. We also have plans to expand the administrative sponsor group to include more deans and directors from partner institutions to further support the project and expand its reach across the country and beyond. We have started meeting with and gaining the support of campus organizations like the first-year experience program at K-State and the School of Nursing at KUMC in order to programmatically embed the learning objects into large-scale programs on our campuses. We are also working toward the procurement of extramural funding dollars to support the expansion of the project and to provide a foundation for a sustainable path forward.

One way that the NLA steering committee regularly engages with the project sponsors is to schedule "State of the NLA" conference calls. For these calls, the steering committee prepares a document containing recent reports on lesson usage, project successes and barriers, and plans for the next semester. These calls typically include discussion about strategic planning efforts and long-term visioning and resource allocation for the project. They are a chance for the steering committee to ask questions, seek guidance, and generally inform our deans and directors about the progress of the project. They help all stakeholders remain engaged and forward thinking over the long term.

For the past five years, the NLA steering committee, consisting of librarians from both founding institutions, K-State and KUMC, has served as the main leadership force behind the project. In 2016, one of the two founding steering committee members from K-State stepped down, and a member from Oklahoma State University (OSU) was asked and agreed to fill that role. As the project grows and brings on new partners, we hope that this steering committee will grow and shift to represent more institutional cultures, goals, and types. Moxley and Maes (2003), the founders of the Great Plains IDEA distance education consortium that has been successfully offering distance programs in the United States for nearly twenty years, claim that interinstitutional alliances require good leadership and a commitment to collaboration and innovation in order to build a network of positive, supportive relationships that support alliance functions. The NLA is moving toward this ideal and is regularly evaluating the need for strong and sustainable leadership.

> ## CRITICAL QUESTIONS
>
> 1. How often will you review both your content and the technology you use to build and host it?
>
> 2. How will you fund the project in the short and long terms?
>
> 3. Do you have the support of administrators at each partner institution?
>
> 4. How can you map your project goals and content to existing standards, outcomes, programs, or initiatives?
>
> 5. Where do you want your project to be in five years and what do you need to do to get there?
>
> 6. What is your project capacity now and with increased funding or staff?
>
> 7. How will you construct your leadership team for sustainability?

References

ACRL (Association of College & Research Libraries). 2016. *Framework for Information Literacy for Higher Education.* www.ala.org/acrl/standards/ilframework.

BusinessDictionary. 2017. S.v. "succession planning." Accessed March 29. www.businessdictionary.com/definition/succession-planning.html.

Great Plains IDEA. 2008. "Model for Inter-institutional Distance Education Academic Alliances." Kansas State University. www.gpidea.org/about/collaboration/model.

Merriam-Webster. 2017. S.v. "stakeholder." Accessed March 29. www.merriam-webster.com/dictionary/stakeholder.

Moxley, Virginia M., and Sue C. Maes. 2003. "The Great Plains Interactive Distance Education Alliance." *Continuing Higher Education Review* 67: 1–10.

Final Thoughts

9

You can't be that kid standing at the top of the waterslide, overthinking it. You have to go down the chute.

—Tina Fey (2011)

The advent of new technology, pedagogy, and profession-wide information literacy documentation, such as the ACRL's *Framework for Information Literacy for Higher Education,* offers the library profession an opportunity for reflection about how and why we teach information literacy. Whether you are struggling with how to engage with the new *Framework,* have taken a new instructional leadership role within your institution, or are simply interested in collaborative learning object design, take time to thoughtfully consider your goals, resources, and energy to embark on a new project.

There are many ways to go about project management, instructional design, and collaborative partnerships, and this manual represents one path that was successful for the New Literacies Alliance project partners. We encourage you to take from this work the sections and processes that will help you and your team build meaningful information literacy instruction. The advantage of a manual format to describe the work of the NLA is to allow you to start your collaborative design process with an existing infrastructure or framework in place. If after reading this manual you determine that the processes and challenges presented here represent too great a burden for you or your team yet you still wish to build information literacy learning objects collaboratively, the NLA is always looking for new partners. Contact one of the authors to learn more about how you or your institution can become a partner.

The following appendixes provide resources that we and others have found helpful in our design work. They are not exhaustive, and the authors encourage active participation in conferences, webinars, and other professional development opportunities where you are able to engage with other librarians and educators within the context of instructional design. If you succeed in your design efforts, and even if you do not (perhaps especially if you do not), share your experiences and best practices with the community so we can all benefit from our collective creative efforts.

Collaborative learning object design is challenging, enlightening, and rewarding, and we hope that by exploring the chapters in this manual you come away equipped with the tools and foundation necessary to delve into this process. We wish you luck and hope that you find as much success and gratification as we have throughout our years building the New Literacies Alliance.

Reference

Fey, Tina. 2011. *Bossypants.* New York: Little Brown.

Appendixes

NLA Self-Study (2012)

Please indicate the resources your institution could contribute to a collaboration in each area.

Goal: Scalable, leveling research modules that can be used by each institution for their own purposes

1. Human resources skill sets

    ☐ Programmers
    ☐ Instructional designers
    ☐ Curriculum specialist
    ☐ Content
    ☐ Writers
    ☐ Project manager
    ☐ Assessment
    ☐ Grant writing
    ☐ Usability testing
    ☐ Other technical skills: how to implement on campus, knowledge of online learning on campus/learning management systems
    ☐ Communication and marketing/outreach
    ☐ "Talent" for audio and video recording
    ☐ Media production: video, audio
    ☐ Cloud knowledge
    ☐ Advocates

2. Technological resources

    ☐ Server space/cloud
    ☐ Learning management system

☐ Capacity to buy software (do you have a budget range?)

☐ Existing software

☐ Private, shared space for the build

3. Production resources

☐ Cameras

☐ Recording studios

☐ Microphones

☐ Editing software

☐ Editing equipment

4. What content?

☐ Scripts

☐ Tutorials

☐ LibGuides

☐ Syllabi

☐ Widgets

5. Can you stop doing anything/redirect efforts?

APPENDIX

B

Steering Committee Responsibilities

Broad functions of the NLA steering committee:

- Set the tone for the project.
- Communicate with and enact directives from the NLA sponsors group (deans and directors of the steering committee libraries).
- Represent their institutions/states/regions and other similar institutions during decision making and planning.
- Determine procedural and managerial oversight of the project.
- Identify resource needs and potential sources (funds, staff, technology, etc.).

Regular duties of the NLA steering committee:

- Meet weekly to discuss project business.
- Set agendas for working group calls and meetings (one per month and twice per year, respectively).
- Communicate with the project's small groups to help with goal setting and maintain momentum.
- Hold ad hoc meetings with NLA sponsors to report on activity and set goals (usually two to three meetings per year).
- Perform new member outreach and communicate with interested institutions.
- Write annual thank-you notes to project team members.

Examples of special projects led by the NLA steering committee:

- Invitations to present and publish about the project.
- Grant writing.
- Workshops for project partners or interested individuals.
- Collaborations with other organizations to promote the work being done.
- Submissions for awards/recognition.
- Lesson submission into content repositories.

Time commitment:

- Standing weekly meetings (typically two to three times per month, virtual).
- Sponsors meetings (two to three times per year, virtual).
- Attendance at working group calls and meetings (one per month and twice per year, respectively, virtual).
- Investment of two to three hours per week, on average, depending on what projects are going on.

Benefits and professional development:

- National and international publications and presentations.
- Possibility of national awards and recognition.
- Grant-writing experience.
- Leadership, strategic planning, and project management experience.
- High-level interinstitutional collaboration experience.
- Opportunities to advocate for their institutions' needs in greater detail.

Intent to Plan Document

Notice of Intent for Program Planning

This agreement is entered into by _____ for the purpose of planning a potential interinstitutional digital instruction program in information literacy.

The partner Universities/organizations in this program planning initiative are:

1. Kansas State University Libraries
2. The University of Kansas Medical Center Dykes Library
3. Institution C
4. Institution D
5. Institution E

It is understood that additional parties may be invited to join this cooperative effort.

_____ University/organization agrees to participate in the planning process. By affixing the appropriate signatures to this document, _____ Library/organization agrees to support faculty participating in the planning of the digital instruction program. A Memorandum of Agreement pertaining to the delivery and maintenance of this program will be created between the Consortium and the University/organization. It is understood that at any time in the planning process or at the conclusion of the planning process, participants may withdraw from the program initiative.

Signatures   Date:_____

Program Faculty _____

Program Department Head _____

Library/Organization Administrator _____

Storyboard Template

Lesson Plan Storyboard Template

This template is meant to help you think through a lesson as it will appear online, and as a student will interact with it. It is meant to be a guide rather than a rule. The work you have completed in steps 1–4 will inform everything you write here. You will deliver this document to the Instructional Designers to begin the content adaptation process.

Lesson Name, Outcome, and Description

[Lesson Name:] The name of the lesson

[Lesson Outcome:] The lesson learning outcome

[Lesson Description:]

Summarize what this lesson is all about. As succinctly as possible (one/two sentences each), answer the following questions:
  —What is the essence of this lesson?
  —Why is this important?
  —How does it relate to students' lives?
  —How will the learning outcome be achieved?
  —What content skills are necessary for the student to succeed? (Insert content skills from step 2 of the Outcomes and Lesson Plans Worksheet)

Take this step as an opportunity to organize your thoughts.

Part 1: Introduction to the Lesson/ Background Information

Set the stage for the lesson by providing context. This section could address questions such as these:
  —What is the student going to learn?
  —Explain or define terms and concepts that students need to know about in order to progress through the lesson successfully.
  —What previous knowledge does the learner need in order to successfully complete the lesson?

 **Part 2: The Story Rises—Making It Relevant to Students' Lives**

Relate the information given in Part 1 to the lives of learners and students. Think about how the information provided at the outset of the lesson affects students at present and in the future. Make them curious about the lesson content, and give them an opportunity to want to explore what follows.

 **Part 2A: A Moment of Reflection**

*At this point, give learners a chance to pause and to reflect on the personal importance of learning about this content. This part is vital in helping learners to appreciate **why** they need to know about this. Ask a question, create a poll, or give a hypothetical scenario that learners should contemplate and respond to.*

Part 3: Stating the Problem

Parts 3 and 3A constitute the core of the instructional content of the lesson. After helping students understand why they need to know about the content of this lesson, deliver the actual lesson content here. Often, the instructional content will revolve around and expound on a current problem or issue. Closely base this content on your stated skills and learning outcome:

    —What should the learners be able to do after completing this lesson?

    —What do learners need to know in order to do this?

Part 3 will likely exceed other parts in length and detail.

Part 3A: Solving the Problem (Bridge)

After explaining the pertinent issue or problem, provide guidance as to how this problem might be solved. Sometimes, there is a clear answer to the solution; other times, the answer might just be one of many (such as lessons dealing with ethical questions and issues). Just like a story, there must be a bridge between the stated problem and the climax.

Part 4: The Lesson Climax

At this point, the learner should be given the opportunity to apply, integrate, and demonstrate understanding of newly gained concepts and knowledge. How can the learner apply this new knowledge? Provide a conceptual idea as to how one might test the learner's ability to transfer gained knowledge to new problems.

(Optional): List up to three practical applications through which learners could demonstrate mastery of content in an online environment.

New Literacies Alliance © 2013
mobile page

Part 4A: Applying the Solution

In a story, the main characters usually spend some time reflecting on the climax events and determining how they shape the rest of their story. Provide learners a bridge between the solution to the lesson problem and actually applying the solution in a real-world scenario.

New Literacies Alliance © 2013
mobile page

Part 5: Assessment

In part 5, review the lesson outcome and the content skills, and then write three possible quiz questions that measure the successful achievement of the outcome.

Conclusion

Conclude with a brief statement that summarizes what the student has accomplished by going through the lesson.

Credits

Cite all references for lesson content in APA style. These will be made into a PDF document linked from the lesson.

Learning Object Rubric

	Needs Editing	Ready to Go	Comments
Learning Object Length			
Learning objects are < 8-15 minutes long.			
Outcomes			
Outcomes checklist has been successfully completed. [See chapter 3.]			
Learning Activities			
All activities are necessary and lead to the outcome.			
Reviewer is able to envision the activities based upon descriptions.			
Storyboard Structure and Content			
Introduction defines new terms and provides adequate context.			
The relevancy of content to students' lives is clear.			
The problem to be solved by mastery of content is presented.			
The main activity (climax) allows students the opportunity to demonstrate their learning.			
The resolution allows students to reflect on learning and content.			
Assessment			
Assessment is provided.			
Outcome is directly assessed.			
Assessment is completely automated.			
Preassessment is included for gating or differentiation.			
Students are provided with feedback for correct and incorrect responses.			
Assessment Criteria			
Pass-fail and/or grading criteria are set.			
Attribution and Copyright			
Attribution/references are complete.			
Copyright permissions have been obtained (if necessary).			
Your author's rights are preserved (© or CC).			

NLA Talking Points (2013)

Founding Principles

- This project supports individual institution/organizational goals and aligns with the Kansas Board of Regents' Foresight 2020 initiative that highlights the need for transferable lifelong learning skills.

- Eventually, we hope partner institutions can use this content as a leveling platform to ensure all students entering and leaving college in Kansas have the same skill set. This will allow for more individualized, intensive face-to-face library instruction, as in-class students will already have the foundational skills we typically cover in a one-shot session.

- Because we will not be busy trying to re-create online modules or teach/reteach foundational principles of research, our instruction programs will become more sustainable, allowing instruction librarians to focus on critically important issues like assessment, engagement, and faculty collaboration.

- The need for online instruction is ever more important as our student populations are comprised of higher percentages of distance students and students who prefer to learn in digital environments. Many students cannot or do not physically come to the library for instruction or services, and this project addresses the need for instruction to this population.

- Why create the NLA and not simply reuse EMPOWER, Microsoft's Digital Learning Content, or other information literacy programs or clearinghouses (MERLOT, ANTS, etc.)? To do the following:

  o Develop a common curriculum across Kansas's state institutions.

  o Provide competency- and skills-based instruction (instruction by design or "backward instruction").

o Pioneer a new approach and a new perspective on trans- or metaliteracies (data, information, numerical, evaluative, reading, digital, etc.).

o Provide assessment structure and data collection across institutions.

Pedagogy

- Online content will be gated and presented in a "dashboard" so that students are presented with only content they have not yet mastered. This will hopefully prevent fatigue and boredom, while allowing students to see their progress within the overall architecture of the content.

- Content will be delivered asynchronously in a variety of formats, including images, videos, case studies, and interactive activities. This will allow for more differentiated learning and for students to master skills at their own pace.

- This project supports the "flipped classroom" approach, allowing students to move through foundational content at their own pace, while using face-to-face contact time in the library for more personalized instruction and assistance, based on student need. In this way, traditional library instruction is supplemented and enhanced.

- The content will begin with a core skill level but will eventually be scaffolded to include multiple skill and knowledge levels, including the K–12 population.

- Lesson content will be "chunked" so that one learning outcome is paired with one activity and related assessments, taking no longer than eight to fifteen minutes to complete. This process will prove optimal for online learners with finite time and attention spans.

- Eventually, gaming elements will be incorporated (such as badges, leaderboards, cross-departmental/institutional competitions, etc.) to engage the generation of gamers already arriving on our campuses.

Technology

- We hope to create an adaptive platform that delivers content based on student skill level and interaction with the system. Adaptive platforms allow for a differentiated approach to online instruction: in addition to students moving through content at their own pace, they will have a choice about the way they consume that content.

- We chose the SoftChalk Cloud (SCC) learning management system to house and deliver content. SCC allows for multi-institution collaboration, includes a wide variety of built-in interactive activities, and contains a robust assessment suite through which we can assess student learning across institutions.

- The built-in assessment suite will allow us to assess student learning through mastery of learning outcomes and to assess the system itself.

- SoftChalk Cloud is optimized for mobile environments and will allow participation for the increasing number of learners who use mobile devices to access learning systems. SCC utilizes HTML5 and non-flash-based interactivity that is accessible across operating systems and devices.

- The system will gather learner analytics as students move through the content. Analysis of the data will allow for greater customization of content and a higher-quality product than can be achieved with other systems.

APPENDIX
G

Rapid Prototyping Test Report

Prototype 3 Feedback

Three undergraduate students all between eighteen and twenty-five years old

	Student 1	Student 2	Student 3
On a scale of 1-4, 4 being very confident that they understood the content of the lessons, the students answered thusly:	4	4	4

Access Matters

	Student 1	Student 2	Student 3	*Average*
Time to go through the lesson:	14:40	22:00	19:40	18.46

ASSESSMENTS RIGHT OR WRONG

	Student 1	Student 2	Student 3
Poll answer:	Could not find the information needed on a website.	Missed important or fun events because you didn't know about them.	Could not find the information you needed on a website.
Max scenario question:	Partially correct (chose b, c, d, f).	Partially correct (chose b, c, d, f), tried again and got the right answer.	Partially correct (chose b, c, d, f), tried again and chose all options.
Case Study ordering 1:	Correct	Correct	Correct
Case Study ordering 2:	Correct	Correct	Correct

(Cont.)

	Student 1	Student 2	Student 3
Short Answer 1:	"I would do as Yoon did in the second situation, where she went to the library, even though it was far away. It is important to have recent data for the most accurate information."	"I would have called the local college to see if there was a way for them to send certain documents or copies to me. If not, I would have driven ninety minutes to the college to do my own research."	"If I were in the same situation as Yoon, I would most likely do the same as her. I would look to find a ride to the college, so that way my information is the most up-to-date it can be and my chances of getting my business started most successful."
Matching 1:	Correct	Correct	Correct
Short Answer 2:	"Mobile sites not being available. I use my phone primarily for everything and may miss out on important information because I cannot access it. I overcome this by using my laptop as needed."	"I'm not quite up-to-date on political standings of candidates for government positions in my home state, and I think that is because of the lack of easily available information. I will probably check local newspapers and news channels and websites to see if there is any more information I could gather."	"One knowledge barrier that I currently face is the information I am searching for being organized by what I like and what is most popular, instead of what is most helpful and most relevant."

Individual Feedback

Student 1	Student 2	Student 3
The videos were really good. Sometimes presentations are really dated and gross, and these ones were good and easy to listen to and understand. The questions weren't overly difficult but still got the information across. Wasn't so specific that you couldn't comprehend what they were asking. (Not too hard, not too easy.) Didn't like: Kind of boring to look at because there aren't lots of fun colors. It wasn't too long which is good. I didn't know that libraries have to pay for database access like someone else would. I understood that Facebook makes ads just for you, but I learned a little bit more about each one [category] specifically.	[Poll results took a long time to load.] I would just assume that was broken. It wasn't overly difficult in the sense of the amount of information thrown at you at one time. They worded the questions in a way that made you think deeper about it rather than just answering immediately. It was also fairly interactive with the way that the questions were set up. Didn't like: Could have been more instruction going from page to page. This was a little confusing trying to figure out if I needed to go on, do more, go back, etc. Make the supporting text bigger to keep us from going straight to the interactive elements.	I like that you are able to check your answers. On the one that I got incorrect it told me why I got it incorrect. It wasn't super wordy which was nice. I didn't think it was that bad. I would have missed the question under the scenario if you hadn't been here. Nothing really too wrong with it. Although the first set of questions was frustrating because I got it wrong, but I think I misread it. I think it was pretty easy to understand what you should be doing. I didn't realize that search engines were organized by the most popular. I knew they varied a little bit but not why they varied. <div align="right">(Cont.)</div>

Student 1	Student 2	Student 3
I chose the govt. scenario because that's the one I know the least about. Would not go back and look at the other two scenarios unless it was required. I wouldn't change anything—I think it's pretty good. Good for a range of students.	I already had an understanding of information barriers since I've done a bunch of research in my major (Kinesiology). But just having all of the information compressed or compiled into this, I was able to structure my thoughts a little better in this than I would have been able to do on my own. I chose the govt. option since I am already familiar with academic research and well-being. When I read well-being I thought that might mean physical well-being and I'm already on top of that because of my major. I wanted to go to that [well-being] but I thought govt. could be an interesting subject.	I chose the government one because I am a business major and I wanted to see what it had to do with that. Government stuff is pretty interesting. I feel pretty comfortable with the well-being stuff.

Action Items

Make the first Carter video larger on the page.

Find a new flashcard activity to plug in, or use the same format as the "Scholarship" lesson for this component. Remove net neutrality flashcard and replace with one of the other matching pairs.

Check on page bookmark hopping—when using the back/continue links, user does not land at the top of the page.

Turn current Google poll into either a SoftChalk poll (which are finally working again) or a Qualtrics poll since none of them actually saw the poll results in the current form. Also change the <iframe> width/length so they can see the whole thing without scrolling.

Add feedback for incorrect answers in the Max scenario question.

Crop video in the Max scenario right before FOI (Freedom of Information) law section and reload into the Google form.

Make navigation between scenarios and pages more explicit.

Take off the requirements for questions in the Google forms. Change the <iframes> for these scenarios so they can see everything in the scenario without scrolling. Add instructions in each form right before the submit button, so they know they can go back and look at the other scenarios by hitting back or continue on. Fix navigation in each form.

Superimpose the text of Yoon's case study onto the extra space in that image to get it out of table format and to help it look a little sleeker.

Try to streamline content to shorten the lesson. Consider removing poll or short answer questions.

We need a little blurb about each scenario before they choose to help them understand what they will be looking at depending on what they choose. I am thinking something like a one-liner for each.

Cartoonize the yoga image, and make this group of three images more infographic-y.

Secure permissions from Carter Foundation to use the videos and the AMA (American Medical Association) video in the Geraldine scenario.

Add more scorable questions (multiple choice, drag-and-drop, matching, etc.).

All of them chose the government option. Do we need to rearrange these to see if they choose differently?

Shorten the short answer boxes by a hard return in the middle of the question text.

Check for ADA compliance.

Rapid Prototyping Student Response Form

Instructions

This survey is part of an ongoing process to evaluate the functionality and usability of the New Literacies Alliance online learning modules. Your help in completing this survey will assist us in the continuing development and improvement of the project. All responses you provide will remain anonymous.

1. I am a/an:
   - a. Undergraduate
   - b. Graduate Student
   - c. Faculty
   - d. Staff
   - e. Other

2. To which age group do you belong?
   - a. Under 18
   - b. 18–20
   - c. 21–25
   - d. 26–30
   - e. 31–45
   - f. 46–60
   - g. 61+

3. On a scale of 0–4 (with 0 being not confident and 4 being very confident), how confident are you that you understood the content of the lesson?
   - a. 0
   - b. 1
   - c. 2
   - d. 3
   - e. 4

4. What did you like about the lesson? Why?

5. What did you not like about the lesson or wish could be changed? Why?

6. Do you have any other comments, thoughts, ideas, or concerns?

7. Do you feel you learned something valuable from the lesson? If so, what did you learn and why was it valuable? If not, what do you wish the lesson would have discussed instead?

Thank you for participating in our usability test.

Checklists and Critical Questions

Throughout a collaborative design process, there are many skills to cultivate, steps to consider, and questions to ask. The following represents a summary of these elements derived from the chapters in this manual. Check off the elements below as you read through each chapter and address each step, or question. Not every element must be checked off for every project to be successful but they serve as a useful guide to help walk you through the process of collaborative design.

CHAPTER 1

The Case for Sharing Instruction

Critical Questions

- ☐ Do you have the staffing, expertise, time, and other resources to create library instruction on your own?
- ☐ Will it benefit your library/institution/patrons to collaborate on library instruction?
- ☐ What are the barriers to collaboration that you foresee?

CHAPTER 2

Getting Started

Checklist

- ☐ Conduct a self-study.
- ☐ Research existing collaborations.
- ☐ Identify and contact potential collaborators.
- ☐ Establish project goals.
- ☐ Confirm collaborator expectations.
- ☐ Identify leaders.

Critical Questions

- ☐ What are your goals?
- ☐ Are your goals flexible enough to accommodate the needs of other institutions?
- ☐ How would working with other institutions help you achieve your goals?
- ☐ How could you contribute to a collaboration?
- ☐ Does your library and/or university administration support interinstitutional collaborations?
- ☐ Can you share resources across institutions?
- ☐ Is there an existing project that meets your needs that you can join?
- ☐ Can you combine resources with anyone else in a meaningful way?
- ☐ Who is the audience for the learning objects?
- ☐ What will students be able to accomplish when they finish your learning objects?
- ☐ How will the learning objects be integrated into student learning?
- ☐ What will the final product look like?
- ☐ What roles do you need to fill on your project?
- ☐ Who will lead your project?

CHAPTER 3

Creating the Learning Experience

Checklist

- ☐ Identify content creators.
- ☐ Organize teams.
- ☐ Select guiding activities for teams.
- ☐ Choose a pedagogical approach.
- ☐ Select an outcomes formula.
- ☐ Identify competencies.
- ☐ Set the structure of learning objects (templates).
- ☐ Customize an evaluation rubric.
- ☐ List creatable learning activities.

Critical Questions

- ☐ Are team members clear about the central purpose and vision for the work?
- ☐ Are teams facilitated with teamwork activities (Liberating Structures) to complete the work?
- ☐ What is the student going to learn?

☐ Why is this content important to the learners?

☐ Will the content be covered broadly or in depth?

☐ What audience level is targeted?

☐ What specifically do you want students to be able to do *after* completing the learning object?

☐ What skills or knowledge is necessary for the student to be a competent practitioner?

☐ What level of mastery on the novice-to-expert scale is practically needed for this particular outcome and at this time?

☐ How will you observe students demonstrating knowledge or understanding of this content? What evidence will best show you that they "got it."

☐ What online activities will you provide in the learning object to teach the content and prepare the student for the assessment?

☐ What are the criteria for mastery? How will you know that the student has done this well or reached a level of proficiency?

☐ Are the instructional librarians familiar with learning object writing styles and templates?

CHAPTER 4

The Design Process

Checklist

☐ Choose a developmental model.

☐ Create a style guide.

☐ Determine testing and reporting procedures.

☐ Determine learning object review process.

☐ Submit IRB (institutional review board) applications for testing.

Critical Questions

☐ What instructional development model will work best for your team?

☐ How many learning objects can you reasonably complete per year with your current project staff and using your chosen development model?

☐ What style parameters are critical to the success and branding of your project?

☐ Do you plan to publish the results of your project and, specifically, the results of student/patron testing?

☐ How will you test your learning objects, including recruiting students/patrons?

☐ What will your final reviews consist of and whom will you ask to help with each aspect?

Implementation

Checklist

- ☐ Ascertain if and how to obtain official approval to implement your project at collaborating institutions.
- ☐ Identify and record internal and external deadlines.
- ☐ Establish and record timelines for completing the implementation process.
- ☐ Identify partners outside the project team.
- ☐ Conduct a soft launch to test learning objects in a controlled environment.
- ☐ Use results of soft launch to modify learning objects/project.
- ☐ Develop marketing/educational resources.
- ☐ Develop pedagogical guidance.
- ☐ Initiate assessment of initial implementation.

Critical Questions

- ☐ What types of approval or permissions are necessary in order to implement your project?
- ☐ What models and institutional resources exist to help you navigate the approval process?
- ☐ What information or resources can be shared between institutions to facilitate gaining approval?
- ☐ Whom do you need to work with outside the project team in order to implement the learning objects?
- ☐ What deadlines do you have to meet?
- ☐ How long do you anticipate it will take to implement your project?
- ☐ How will the data collected be managed?
- ☐ What do you need to learn from a soft rollout?
- ☐ How does your project help faculty/students do whatever they are doing, better?
- ☐ Who are your audiences?
- ☐ What information do they need to know?
- ☐ What pedagogical guidance do your teaching partners need in order to use the learning objects?
- ☐ What logistical information/resources do your partners need in order to use the learning objects?
- ☐ How will you troubleshoot or provide technical support for the learning objects?

CHAPTER 6

Technical Parameters

Checklist

☐ Determine where learning objects are to be hosted.

☐ Ensure ADA (Americans with Disabilities Act) accessibility.

☐ Complete feature/functionality list.

☐ Plan to analyze software.

Critical Questions

☐ Who will need access to the learning objects and how will they use them?

☐ Are you going to collect assessment data and, if yes, where will you store it?

☐ Where will the learning objects need to live in order to facilitate access and assessment?

☐ Does the product you are considering meet ADA and Section 508 requirements?

☐ What technical constraints are you working under, such as available IT support and technical skills of your project staff?

☐ What are the minimum features and functionalities you need in a software package to achieve your project goals?

☐ How much can you afford to spend up front and annually on software and hosting?

CHAPTER 7

Assessment

Checklist

☐ Identify student learning tools.

☐ Identify project assessment tools.

☐ Plan for implementing assessments.

☐ Set scoring options and technologies.

☐ Establish a process for sharing/providing scores.

☐ Plan for closing the loop and demonstrating value.

Critical Questions

☐ Do faculty report that the learning objects augment their course content?

☐ How do learning object outcomes tie into existing standards and competencies?

- ☐ Are the learning objects you build really teaching students to master outcomes you set?
- ☐ How will the learning object be scored? (Will it be formatively or summatively assessed?)
- ☐ How can student progress be tracked from one learning object to another, one course to another, and even one institution to another?
- ☐ How will you assess the learning objects and what data will guide you in improving them?
- ☐ How can a peer-review model improve project deliverables?
- ☐ How can librarians demonstrate that learning objects improve departmental, programmatic, or university outcomes?

Long-Term Planning

Checklist

- ☐ Establish a content and technology review schedule.
- ☐ Create a funding plan with your leadership team.
- ☐ Map your project's existing standards, outcomes, programs, and initiatives.
- ☐ Establish a leadership succession plan.

Critical Questions

- ☐ How often will you review both your content and the technology you use to build and host it?
- ☐ How will you fund the project in the short and long terms?
- ☐ Do you have the support of administrators at each partner institution?
- ☐ How can you map your project goals and content to existing standards, outcomes, programs, or initiatives?
- ☐ Where do you want your project to be in five years and what do you need to do to get there?
- ☐ What is your project capacity now and with increased funding or staff?
- ☐ How will you construct your leadership team for sustainability?

About the Authors

JOELLE PITTS is Instructional Design Librarian and Associate Professor at Kansas State University Libraries. She leads the award-winning New Literacies Alliance and is responsible for the creation of Web-based learning objects and environments aimed at increasing information literacy. Her research interests include distance education and e-learning design, library user experience, academic collaboration, and the design and implementation of games-based learning environments. She has written extensively and presented at the local, national, and international levels.

SARA K. KEARNS is Academic Services Librarian and Associate Professor at Kansas State University Libraries. While serving as department head for K-State Libraries' Undergraduate and Community Services Departments she became a founding member of the New Literacies Alliance. Kearns earned her PhD in student affairs in higher education, studying first-year college students' perceptions of technology in higher education. She currently serves on a multi-institutional research project to determine the impact of library instruction on the success and retention of first-year college students. She presents and publishes about student success and learning.

HEATHER COLLINS leads the Research and Learning Department at the University of Kansas Medical Center Library. She has been a founding member of the New Literacies Alliance and continues to serve on the steering committee. As a Reynolds Interprofessional Faculty Scholars Fellow and a recent interprofessional NIH grant team member, her research and presentations focus on areas of intersection between disciplines such as metaliteracy, interprofessional education, and competency-based education.

Index